Mometrix
TEST PREPARATION

Regents

Success Strategies
Physics

DEAR FUTURE EXAM SUCCESS STORY

First of all, **THANK YOU** for purchasing Mometrix study materials!

Second, congratulations! You are one of the few determined test-takers who are committed to doing whatever it takes to excel on your exam. **You have come to the right place.** We developed these study materials with one goal in mind: to deliver you the information you need in a format that's concise and easy to use.

In addition to optimizing your guide for the content of the test, we've outlined our recommended steps for breaking down the preparation process into small, attainable goals so you can make sure you stay on track.

We've also analyzed the entire test-taking process, identifying the most common pitfalls and showing how you can overcome them and be ready for any curveball the test throws you.

Standardized testing is one of the biggest obstacles on your road to success, which only increases the importance of doing well in the high-pressure, high-stakes environment of test day. Your results on this test could have a significant impact on your future, and this guide provides the information and practical advice to help you achieve your full potential on test day.

Your success is our success

We would love to hear from you! If you would like to share the story of your exam success or if you have any questions or comments in regard to our products, please contact us at **800-673-8175** or **support@mometrix.com**.

Thanks again for your business and we wish you continued success!

Sincerely,
The Mometrix Test Preparation Team

Printed in the United States of America

Table of Contents

Introduction

Thank you for purchasing this resource! You have made the choice to prepare yourself for a test that could have a huge impact on your future, and this guide is designed to help you be fully ready for test day. Obviously, it's important to have a solid understanding of the test material, but you also need to be prepared for the unique environment and stressors of the test, so that you can perform to the best of your abilities.

For this purpose, the first section that appears in this guide is the **Success Strategies**. We've devoted countless hours to meticulously researching what works and what doesn't, and we've boiled down our findings to the five most impactful steps you can take to improve your performance on the test. We start at the beginning with study planning and move through the preparation process, all the way to the testing strategies that will help you get the most out of what you know when you're finally sitting in front of the test.

We recommend that you start preparing for your test as far in advance as possible. However, if you've bought this guide as a last-minute study resource and only have a few days before your test, we recommend that you skip over the first two Success Strategies since they address a long-term study plan.

If you struggle with **test anxiety**, we strongly encourage you to check out our recommendations for how you can overcome it. Test anxiety is a formidable foe, but it can be beaten, and we want to make sure you have the tools you need to defeat it.

Strategy #1 – Plan Big, Study Small

There's a lot riding on your performance. If you want to ace this test, you're going to need to keep your skills sharp and the material fresh in your mind. You need a plan that lets you review everything you need to know while still fitting in your schedule. We'll break this strategy down into three categories.

Information Organization

Start with the information you already have: the official test outline. From this, you can make a complete list of all the concepts you need to cover before the test. Organize these concepts into groups that can be studied together, and create a list of any related vocabulary you need to learn so you can brush up on any difficult terms. You'll want to keep this vocabulary list handy once you actually start studying since you may need to add to it along the way.

Time Management

Once you have your set of study concepts, decide how to spread them out over the time you have left before the test. Break your study plan into small, clear goals so you have a manageable task for each day and know exactly what you're doing. Then just focus on one small step at a time. When you manage your time this way, you don't need to spend hours at a time studying. Studying a small block of content for a short period each day helps you retain information better and avoid stressing over how much you have left to do. You can relax knowing that you have a plan to cover everything in time. In order for this strategy to be effective though, you have to start studying early and stick to your schedule. Avoid the exhaustion and futility that comes from last-minute cramming!

Study Environment

The environment you study in has a big impact on your learning. Studying in a coffee shop, while probably more enjoyable, is not likely to be as fruitful as studying in a quiet room. It's important to keep distractions to a minimum. You're only planning to study for a short block of time, so make the most of it. Don't pause to check your phone or get up to find a snack. It's also important to **avoid multitasking**. Research has consistently shown that multitasking will make your studying dramatically less effective. Your study area should also be comfortable and well-lit so you don't have the distraction of straining your eyes or sitting on an uncomfortable chair.

The time of day you study is also important. You want to be rested and alert. Don't wait until just before bedtime. Study when you'll be most likely to comprehend and remember. Even better, if you know what time of day your test will be, set that time aside for study. That way your brain will be used to working on that subject at that specific time and you'll have a better chance of recalling information.

Finally, it can be helpful to team up with others who are studying for the same test. Your actual studying should be done in as isolated an environment as possible, but the work of organizing the information and setting up the study plan can be divided up. In between study sessions, you can discuss with your teammates the concepts that you're all studying and quiz each other on the details. Just be sure that your teammates are as serious about the test as you are. If you find that your study time is being replaced with social time, you might need to find a new team.

Strategy #2 – Make Your Studying Count

You're devoting a lot of time and effort to preparing for this test, so you want to be absolutely certain it will pay off. This means doing more than just reading the content and hoping you can remember it on test day. It's important to make every minute of study count. There are two main areas you can focus on to make your studying count.

Retention

It doesn't matter how much time you study if you can't remember the material. You need to make sure you are retaining the concepts. To check your retention of the information you're learning, try recalling it at later times with minimal prompting. Try carrying around flashcards and glance at one or two from time to time or ask a friend who's also studying for the test to quiz you.

To enhance your retention, look for ways to put the information into practice so that you can apply it rather than simply recalling it. If you're using the information in practical ways, it will be much easier to remember. Similarly, it helps to solidify a concept in your mind if you're not only reading it to yourself but also explaining it to someone else. Ask a friend to let you teach them about a concept you're a little shaky on (or speak aloud to an imaginary audience if necessary). As you try to summarize, define, give examples, and answer your friend's questions, you'll understand the concepts better and they will stay with you longer. Finally, step back for a big picture view and ask yourself how each piece of information fits with the whole subject. When you link the different concepts together and see them working together as a whole, it's easier to remember the individual components.

Finally, practice showing your work on any multi-step problems, even if you're just studying. Writing out each step you take to solve a problem will help solidify the process in your mind, and you'll be more likely to remember it during the test.

Modality

Modality simply refers to the means or method by which you study. Choosing a study modality that fits your own individual learning style is crucial. No two people learn best in exactly the same way, so it's important to know your strengths and use them to your advantage.

For example, if you learn best by visualization, focus on visualizing a concept in your mind and draw an image or a diagram. Try color-coding your notes, illustrating them, or creating symbols that will trigger your mind to recall a learned concept. If you learn best by hearing or discussing information, find a study partner who learns the same way or read aloud to yourself. Think about how to put the information in your own words. Imagine that you are giving a lecture on the topic and record yourself so you can listen to it later.

For any learning style, flashcards can be helpful. Organize the information so you can take advantage of spare moments to review. Underline key words or phrases. Use different colors for different categories. Mnemonic devices (such as creating a short list in which every item starts with the same letter) can also help with retention. Find what works best for you and use it to store the information in your mind most effectively and easily.

Strategy #3 – Practice the Right Way

Your success on test day depends not only on how many hours you put into preparing, but also on whether you prepared the right way. It's good to check along the way to see if your studying is paying off. One of the most effective ways to do this is by taking practice tests to evaluate your progress. Practice tests are useful because they show exactly where you need to improve. Every time you take a practice test, pay special attention to these three groups of questions:

- The questions you got wrong
- The questions you had to guess on, even if you guessed right
- The questions you found difficult or slow to work through

This will show you exactly what your weak areas are, and where you need to devote more study time. Ask yourself why each of these questions gave you trouble. Was it because you didn't understand the material? Was it because you didn't remember the vocabulary? Do you need more repetitions on this type of question to build speed and confidence? Dig into those questions and figure out how you can strengthen your weak areas as you go back to review the material.

Additionally, many practice tests have a section explaining the answer choices. It can be tempting to read the explanation and think that you now have a good understanding of the concept. However, an explanation likely only covers part of the question's broader context. Even if the explanation makes perfect sense, **go back and investigate** every concept related to the question until you're positive you have a thorough understanding.

As you go along, keep in mind that the practice test is just that: practice. Memorizing these questions and answers will not be very helpful on the actual test because it is unlikely to have any of the same exact questions. If you only know the right answers to the sample questions, you won't be prepared for the real thing. **Study the concepts** until you understand them fully, and then you'll be able to answer any question that shows up on the test.

It's important to wait on the practice tests until you're ready. If you take a test on your first day of study, you may be overwhelmed by the amount of material covered and how much you need to learn. Work up to it gradually.

On test day, you'll need to be prepared for answering questions, managing your time, and using the test-taking strategies you've learned. It's a lot to balance, like a mental marathon that will have a big impact on your future. Like training for a marathon, you'll need to start slowly and work your way up. When test day arrives, you'll be ready.

Start with the strategies you've read in the first two Success Strategies—plan your course and study in the way that works best for you. If you have time, consider using multiple study resources to get different approaches to the same concepts. It can be helpful to see difficult concepts from more than one angle. Then find a good source for practice tests. Many times, the test website will suggest potential study resources or provide sample tests.

Practice Test Strategy

If you're able to find at least three practice tests, we recommend this strategy:

UNTIMED AND OPEN-BOOK PRACTICE

Take the first test with no time constraints and with your notes and study guide handy. Take your time and focus on applying the strategies you've learned.

TIMED AND OPEN-BOOK PRACTICE

Take the second practice test open-book as well, but set a timer and practice pacing yourself to finish in time.

TIMED AND CLOSED-BOOK PRACTICE

Take any other practice tests as if it were test day. Set a timer and put away your study materials. Sit at a table or desk in a quiet room, imagine yourself at the testing center, and answer questions as quickly and accurately as possible.

Keep repeating timed and closed-book tests on a regular basis until you run out of practice tests or it's time for the actual test. Your mind will be ready for the schedule and stress of test day, and you'll be able to focus on recalling the material you've learned.

Strategy #4 – Pace Yourself

Once you're fully prepared for the material on the test, your biggest challenge on test day will be managing your time. Just knowing that the clock is ticking can make you panic even if you have plenty of time left. Work on pacing yourself so you can build confidence against the time constraints of the exam. Pacing is a difficult skill to master, especially in a high-pressure environment, so **practice is vital**.

Set time expectations for your pace based on how much time is available. For example, if a section has 60 questions and the time limit is 30 minutes, you know you have to average 30 seconds or less per question in order to answer them all. Although 30 seconds is the hard limit, set 25 seconds per question as your goal, so you reserve extra time to spend on harder questions. When you budget extra time for the harder questions, you no longer have any reason to stress when those questions take longer to answer.

Don't let this time expectation distract you from working through the test at a calm, steady pace, but keep it in mind so you don't spend too much time on any one question. Recognize that taking extra time on one question you don't understand may keep you from answering two that you do understand later in the test. If your time limit for a question is up and you're still not sure of the answer, mark it and move on, and come back to it later if the time and the test format allow. If the testing format doesn't allow you to return to earlier questions, just make an educated guess; then put it out of your mind and move on.

On the easier questions, be careful not to rush. It may seem wise to hurry through them so you have more time for the challenging ones, but it's not worth missing one if you know the concept and just didn't take the time to read the question fully. Work efficiently but make sure you understand the question and have looked at all of the answer choices, since more than one may seem right at first.

Even if you're paying attention to the time, you may find yourself a little behind at some point. You should speed up to get back on track, but do so wisely. Don't panic; just take a few seconds less on each question until you're caught up. Don't guess without thinking, but do look through the answer choices and eliminate any you know are wrong. If you can get down to two choices, it is often worthwhile to guess from those. Once you've chosen an answer, move on and don't dwell on any that you skipped or had to hurry through. If a question was taking too long, chances are it was one of the harder ones, so you weren't as likely to get it right anyway.

On the other hand, if you find yourself getting ahead of schedule, it may be beneficial to slow down a little. The more quickly you work, the more likely you are to make a careless mistake that will affect your score. You've budgeted time for each question, so don't be afraid to spend that time. Practice an efficient but careful pace to get the most out of the time you have.

Test-Taking Strategies

This section contains a list of test-taking strategies that you may find helpful as you work through the test. By taking what you know and applying logical thought, you can maximize your chances of answering any question correctly!

It is very important to realize that every question is different and every person is different: no single strategy will work on every question, and no single strategy will work for every person. That's why we've included all of them here, so you can try them out and determine which ones work best for different types of questions and which ones work best for you.

Question Strategies

⊘ Read Carefully

Read the question and the answer choices carefully. Don't miss the question because you misread the terms. You have plenty of time to read each question thoroughly and make sure you understand what is being asked. Yet a happy medium must be attained, so don't waste too much time. You must read carefully and efficiently.

⊘ Contextual Clues

Look for contextual clues. If the question includes a word you are not familiar with, look at the immediate context for some indication of what the word might mean. Contextual clues can often give you all the information you need to decipher the meaning of an unfamiliar word. Even if you can't determine the meaning, you may be able to narrow down the possibilities enough to make a solid guess at the answer to the question.

⊘ Prefixes

If you're having trouble with a word in the question or answer choices, try dissecting it. Take advantage of every clue that the word might include. Prefixes can be a huge help. Usually, they allow you to determine a basic meaning. *Pre-* means before, *post-* means after, *pro-* is positive, *de-* is negative. From prefixes, you can get an idea of the general meaning of the word and try to put it into context.

⊘ Hedge Words

Watch out for critical hedge words, such as *likely, may, can, often, almost, mostly, usually, generally, rarely*, and *sometimes*. Question writers insert these hedge phrases to cover every possibility. Often an answer choice will be wrong simply because it leaves no room for exception. Be on guard for answer choices that have definitive words such as *exactly* and *always*.

⊘ Switchback Words

Stay alert for *switchbacks*. These are the words and phrases frequently used to alert you to shifts in thought. The most common switchback words are *but, although*, and *however*. Others include *nevertheless, on the other hand, even though, while, in spite of, despite*, and *regardless of*. Switchback words are important to catch because they can change the direction of the question or an answer choice.

✓ Face Value

When in doubt, use common sense. Accept the situation in the problem at face value. Don't read too much into it. These problems will not require you to make wild assumptions. If you have to go beyond creativity and warp time or space in order to have an answer choice fit the question, then you should move on and consider the other answer choices. These are normal problems rooted in reality. The applicable relationship or explanation may not be readily apparent, but it is there for you to figure out. Use your common sense to interpret anything that isn't clear.

Answer Choice Strategies

✓ Answer Selection

The most thorough way to pick an answer choice is to identify and eliminate wrong answers until only one is left, then confirm it is the correct answer. Sometimes an answer choice may immediately seem right, but be careful. The test writers will usually put more than one reasonable answer choice on each question, so take a second to read all of them and make sure that the other choices are not equally obvious. As long as you have time left, it is better to read every answer choice than to pick the first one that looks right without checking the others.

✓ Answer Choice Families

An answer choice family consists of two (in rare cases, three) answer choices that are very similar in construction and cannot all be true at the same time. If you see two answer choices that are direct opposites or parallels, one of them is usually the correct answer. For instance, if one answer choice says that quantity *x* increases and another either says that quantity *x* decreases (opposite) or says that quantity *y* increases (parallel), then those answer choices would fall into the same family. An answer choice that doesn't match the construction of the answer choice family is more likely to be incorrect. Most questions will not have answer choice families, but when they do appear, you should be prepared to recognize them.

✓ Eliminate Answers

Eliminate answer choices as soon as you realize they are wrong, but make sure you consider all possibilities. If you are eliminating answer choices and realize that the last one you are left with is also wrong, don't panic. Start over and consider each choice again. There may be something you missed the first time that you will realize on the second pass.

✓ Avoid Fact Traps

Don't be distracted by an answer choice that is factually true but doesn't answer the question. You are looking for the choice that answers the question. Stay focused on what the question is asking for so you don't accidentally pick an answer that is true but incorrect. Always go back to the question and make sure the answer choice you've selected actually answers the question and is not merely a true statement.

✓ Extreme Statements

In general, you should avoid answers that put forth extreme actions as standard practice or proclaim controversial ideas as established fact. An answer choice that states the "process should be used in certain situations, if..." is much more likely to be correct than one that states the "process should be discontinued completely." The first is a calm rational statement and doesn't even make a definitive, uncompromising stance, using a hedge word *if* to provide wiggle room, whereas the second choice is far more extreme.

⊘ BENCHMARK

As you read through the answer choices and you come across one that seems to answer the question well, mentally select that answer choice. This is not your final answer, but it's the one that will help you evaluate the other answer choices. The one that you selected is your benchmark or standard for judging each of the other answer choices. Every other answer choice must be compared to your benchmark. That choice is correct until proven otherwise by another answer choice beating it. If you find a better answer, then that one becomes your new benchmark. Once you've decided that no other choice answers the question as well as your benchmark, you have your final answer.

⊘ PREDICT THE ANSWER

Before you even start looking at the answer choices, it is often best to try to predict the answer. When you come up with the answer on your own, it is easier to avoid distractions and traps because you will know exactly what to look for. The right answer choice is unlikely to be word-for-word what you came up with, but it should be a close match. Even if you are confident that you have the right answer, you should still take the time to read each option before moving on.

General Strategies

⊘ TOUGH QUESTIONS

If you are stumped on a problem or it appears too hard or too difficult, don't waste time. Move on! Remember though, if you can quickly check for obviously incorrect answer choices, your chances of guessing correctly are greatly improved. Before you completely give up, at least try to knock out a couple of possible answers. Eliminate what you can and then guess at the remaining answer choices before moving on.

⊘ CHECK YOUR WORK

Since you will probably not know every term listed and the answer to every question, it is important that you get credit for the ones that you do know. Don't miss any questions through careless mistakes. If at all possible, try to take a second to look back over your answer selection and make sure you've selected the correct answer choice and haven't made a costly careless mistake (such as marking an answer choice that you didn't mean to mark). This quick double check should more than pay for itself in caught mistakes for the time it costs.

⊘ PACE YOURSELF

It's easy to be overwhelmed when you're looking at a page full of questions; your mind is confused and full of random thoughts, and the clock is ticking down faster than you would like. Calm down and maintain the pace that you have set for yourself. Especially as you get down to the last few minutes of the test, don't let the small numbers on the clock make you panic. As long as you are on track by monitoring your pace, you are guaranteed to have time for each question.

⊘ DON'T RUSH

It is very easy to make errors when you are in a hurry. Maintaining a fast pace in answering questions is pointless if it makes you miss questions that you would have gotten right otherwise. Test writers like to include distracting information and wrong answers that seem right. Taking a little extra time to avoid careless mistakes can make all the difference in your test score. Find a pace that allows you to be confident in the answers that you select.

⊘ KEEP MOVING

Panicking will not help you pass the test, so do your best to stay calm and keep moving. Taking deep breaths and going through the answer elimination steps you practiced can help to break through a stress barrier and keep your pace.

Final Notes

The combination of a solid foundation of content knowledge and the confidence that comes from practicing your plan for applying that knowledge is the key to maximizing your performance on test day. As your foundation of content knowledge is built up and strengthened, you'll find that the strategies included in this chapter become more and more effective in helping you quickly sift through the distractions and traps of the test to isolate the correct answer.

Now that you're preparing to move forward into the test content chapters of this book, be sure to keep your goal in mind. As you read, think about how you will be able to apply this information on the test. If you've already seen sample questions for the test and you have an idea of the question format and style, try to come up with questions of your own that you can answer based on what you're reading. This will give you valuable practice applying your knowledge in the same ways you can expect to on test day.

Good luck and good studying!

Physics

Work, Energy, and Power

Basic Equation for Work

The equation for **work** (W) is $W = \boldsymbol{Fd}$, where $\boldsymbol{F}$ is the force exerted and $\boldsymbol{d}$ is the displacement of the object on which the force is exerted. For the simplest case, when the vectors of force and displacement have the same direction, the work done is equal to the product of the magnitudes of the force and displacement. If this is not the case, then the work may be calculated as $W = \boldsymbol{Fd} \cos \theta$, where θ is the angle between the force and displacement vectors. If force and displacement have the same direction, then work is positive; if they are in opposite directions, however, work is negative; and if they are perpendicular, the work done by the force is zero.

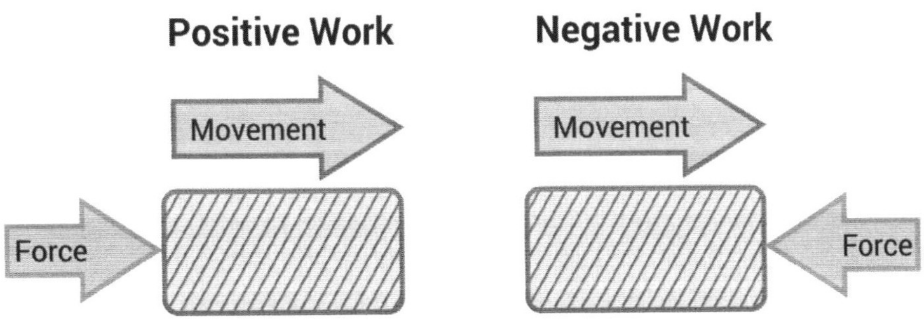

Review Video: Work
Visit mometrix.com/academy and enter code: 681834

For example, if a man pushes a block horizontally across a surface with a constant force of 10 N for a distance of 20 m, the work done by the man is 200 N-m or 200 J. If instead the block is sliding and the man tries to **slow its progress** by pushing against it, his work done is –200 J, since he is pushing in the direction opposite the motion. Also, if the man pushes vertically downward on the block while it slides, his work done is zero, since his force vector is perpendicular to the displacement vector of the block. It is important to note in each of these cases that neither the mass of the block nor the elapsed time is considered when calculating the amount of work done by the man.

Review Video: Push and Pull Forces
Visit mometrix.com/academy and enter code: 104731

Power

Put simply, **power** is the **rate at which work is done**. Power, like work, is a scalar quantity. If we know the amount of work, W, that has been performed in a given amount of time, Δt, then we may find average power, $P_{avg} = \frac{W}{\Delta t}$. If we are instead looking for the instantaneous power, there are two possibilities. If the force on an object is constant, and the object is moving at a constant velocity, then the instantaneous power is the same as the average power. If either the force or the velocity is varying, the instantaneous power should be computed by the equation $P = \boldsymbol{Fv}$, where $\boldsymbol{F}$ and $\boldsymbol{v}$ are the instantaneous force and velocity, respectively. This equation may also be used to compute average power if the force and velocity are constant. Power is typically expressed in joules per second, or watts.

Simple Machines

Simple machines include the pulley, lever, wheel and axle, wedge, inclined plane, and screw. These simple machines have no internal source of energy. More complex or compound machines can be formed from them. Simple machines provide a mechanical advantage and make it easier to accomplish a task. Single or double pulleys allow for easier direction of force. A lever enables a multiplication of force. The wheel and axle allows for movement with less resistance. The inclined plane enables a force less than an object's weight to be used to push it to a greater height. The wedge and screw are forms of the inclined plane. A wedge turns a smaller force working over a greater distance into a larger force. The screw is similar to an incline that is wrapped around a shaft.

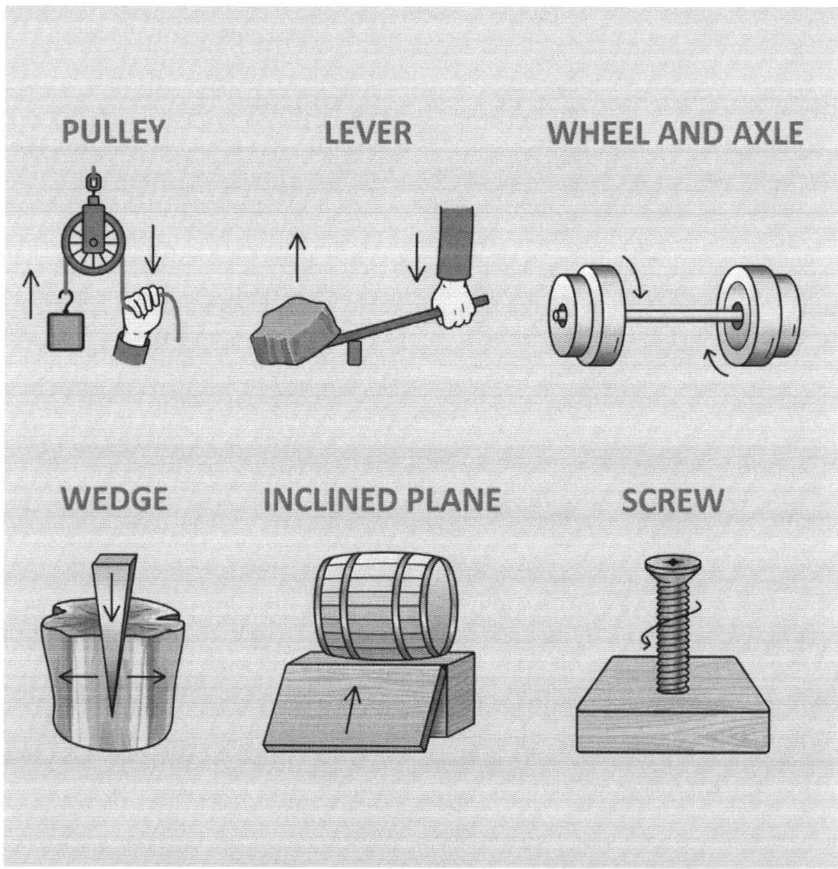

Review Video: Simple Machines
Visit mometrix.com/academy and enter code: 950789

Mechanical Advantage

There is a certain amount of **work** required to move an object that cannot be reduced. However, using one or more simple machines can increase either the distance or force needed. Since work is defined as a force multiplied by a distance, force and distance are inversely proportional.

$$\textbf{Work}_{\textbf{input}} = \textbf{Work}_{\textbf{output}}$$

$$\textbf{force}_{\textbf{input}} \times \textbf{distance}_{\textbf{input}} = \textbf{force}_{\textbf{output}} \times \textbf{distance}_{\textbf{output}}$$

Simple machines can either reduce the amount of input force needed by increasing the input distance or they can reduce the input distance needed by increasing the required input force. The ratio of the output force over the input force is a measure of the **mechanical advantage** of a machine. Due to the inverse relationship between force and distance for these machines, mechanical advantage can also be expressed as the ratio of input distance over the output distance.

$$\textbf{Mechanical Advantage} = \frac{\textbf{force}_{\textbf{output}}}{\textbf{force}_{\textbf{input}}} = \frac{\textbf{distance}_{\textbf{input}}}{\textbf{distance}_{\textbf{output}}}$$

Levers

The **lever** is the most common kind of simple machine. See-saws, shovels, and baseball bats are all examples of levers. There are three classes of levers which are differentiated by the relative orientations of the fulcrum, resistance, and effort. The **fulcrum** is the point at which the lever rotates, the **effort** is the point on the lever where force is applied, and the **resistance** is the part of the lever that acts in response to the effort.

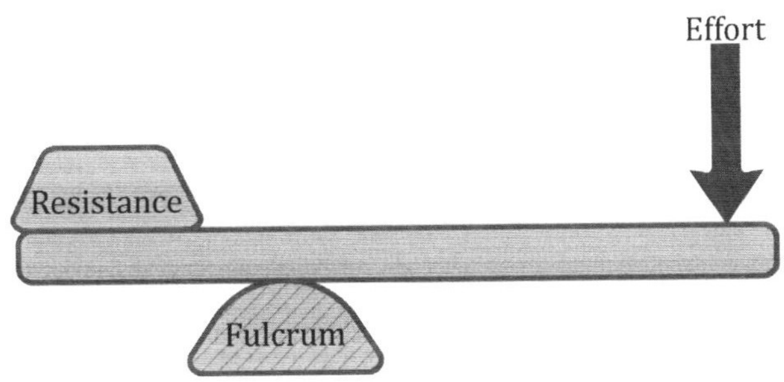

The mechanical advantage of a lever depends on the distances of the effort and resistance from the fulcrum.

$$\textbf{Mechanical Advantage} = \frac{\textbf{effort distance}}{\textbf{resistance distance}}$$

In a **first-class lever**, the fulcrum is between the effort and the resistance. A seesaw is a good example of a first-class lever when effort is applied to force one end up, the other end goes down, and vice versa. The shorter the distance between the fulcrum and the resistance, the easier it will be to move the resistance. As an example, consider whether it is easier to lift another person on a seesaw when they are sitting close to the middle or all the way at the end. A little practice will show you that it is much more difficult to lift a person the farther away he or she is on the see-saw.

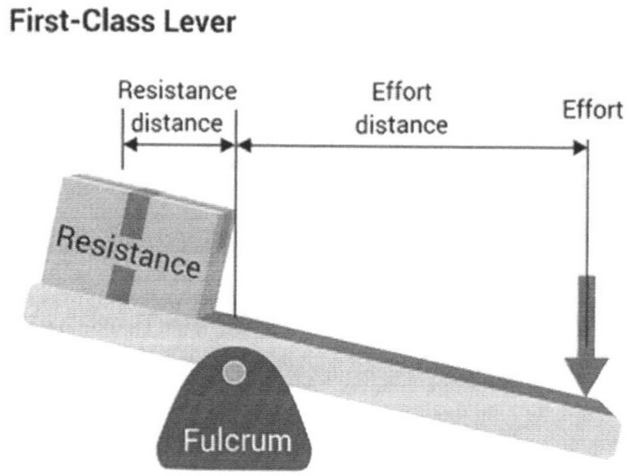

In a **second-class lever**, the resistance is in between the fulcrum and the effort. While a first-class lever is able to increase force and distance through mechanical advantage, a second-class lever is only able to increase force. A common example of a second-class lever is the wheelbarrow; the force exerted by your hand at one end of the wheelbarrow is magnified at the load. Basically, with a second-class lever, you are trading distance for force; by moving your end of the wheelbarrow a bit farther, you produce greater force at the load.

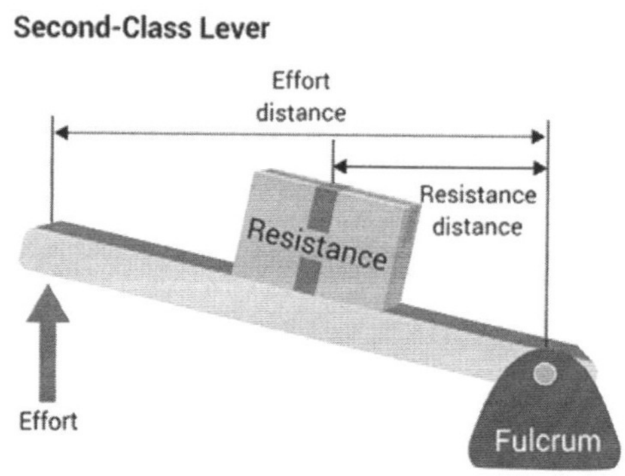

Third-class levers are used to produce greater distance. In a third-class lever, the force is applied in between the fulcrum and the resistance. A baseball bat is a classic example of a third-class lever; the bottom of the bat, below where you grip it, is considered the fulcrum. The end of the bat, where the ball is struck, is the resistance. By exerting effort at the base of the bat, close to the fulcrum, you are able to make the end of the bat fly quickly through the air. The closer your hands are to the base of the bat, the faster you will be able to make the other end of the bat travel.

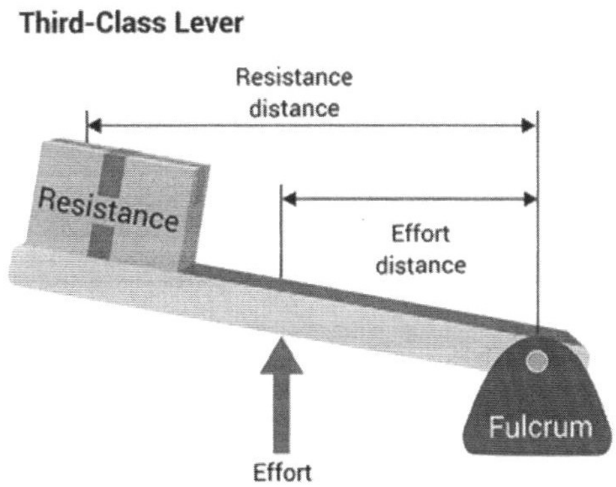

Review Video: Levers
Visit mometrix.com/academy and enter code: 103910

WHEEL AND AXLE

Another basic arrangement that makes use of simple machines is called the wheel and axle. When most people think of a wheel and axle, they immediately envision an automobile tire. The steering wheel of the car, however, operates on the same mechanical principle, namely that the force required to move the center of a circle is much greater than the force required to move the outer rim of a circle. When you turn the steering wheel, you are essentially using a second-class lever by increasing the output force by increasing the input distance. The force required to turn the wheel from the outer rim is much less than would be required to turn the wheel from its center.

The equation for the mechanical advantage of a wheel and axle is:

$$\textbf{Mechanical Advantage} = \frac{\textbf{radius}_{\textbf{wheel}}}{\textbf{radius}_{\textbf{axle}}}$$

For instance, a steering wheel with a radius of 12 inches has a greater mechanical advantage than a steering wheel with a radius of 10 inches; the same amount of force exerted on the rim of each wheel will produce greater force on the axle of the larger wheel.

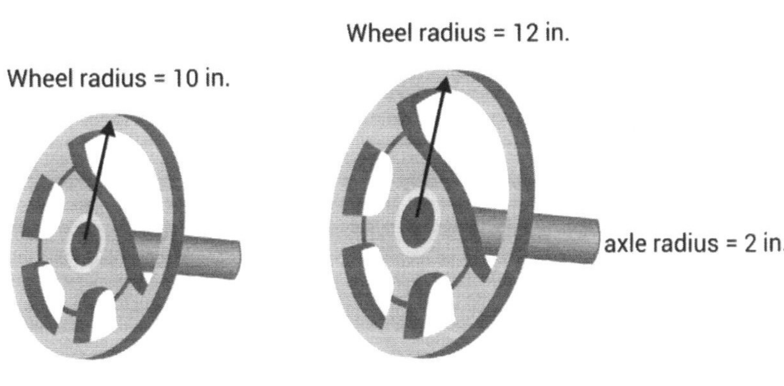

Thus, the mechanical advantage for each is:

$$\frac{10 \text{ inches}}{2 \text{ inches}} = 5 \qquad \frac{12 \text{ inches}}{2 \text{ inches}} = 6$$

Review Video: Wheel and Axle
Visit mometrix.com/academy and enter code: 574045

PULLEYS

The pulley is a simple machine in which a rope is carried by the rotation of a wheel. Another name for a pulley is a block. Pulleys are typically used to allow the force to be directed from a convenient location. For instance, imagine you are given the task of lifting a heavy and tall bookcase. Rather than tying a rope to the bookcase and trying to lift it, it would make sense to tie a pulley system to a rafter above the bookcase and run the rope through it, so that you could pull down on the rope and lift the bookcase. Pulling down allows you to incorporate your weight (normal force) into the act of lifting, thereby making it easier.

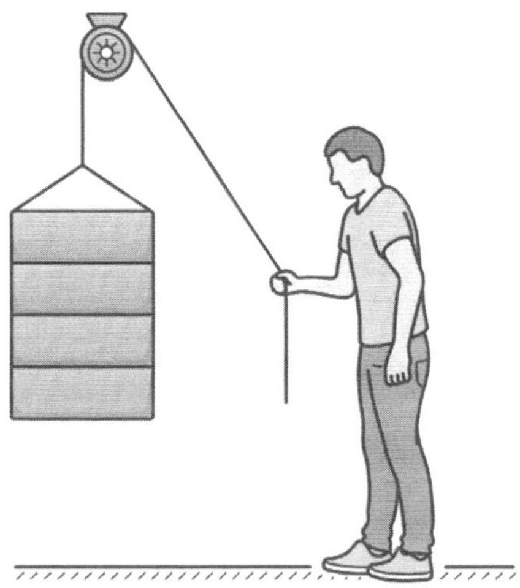

If there is just one pulley above the bookcase, you have created a first-class lever that will not diminish the amount of force that needs to be applied to lift the bookcase. There is another way to use a pulley, however, that can make the job of lifting a heavy object considerably easier. First, tie the rope directly to the rafter. Then, attach a pulley to the top of the bookcase and run the rope through it. If you can then stand so that you are above the bookcase, you will have a much easier time lifting this heavy object. This is because the weight of the bookcase is now being distributed: half of it is acting on the rafter, and half of it is acting on you. In other words, this arrangement allows you to lift an object with half the force. This simple pulley system, therefore, has a mechanical advantage of 2. Note that in this arrangement, the unfixed pulley is acting like a second-class lever. The price you pay for your mechanical advantage is that whatever distance you raise your end of the rope, the bookcase will only be lifted half as much.

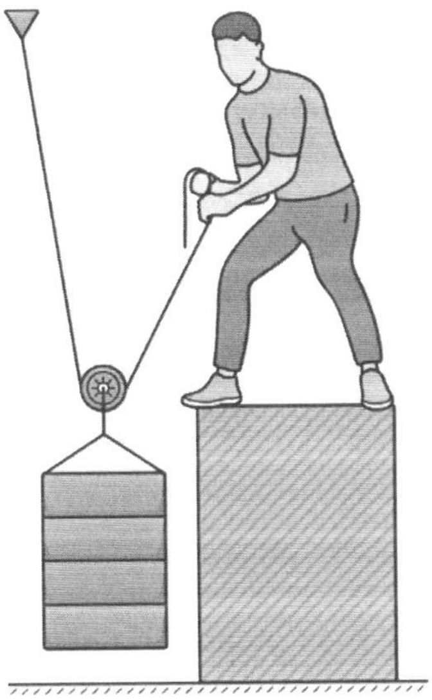

Of course, it might be difficult for you to find a place high enough to enact this system. If this is the case, you can always tie another pulley to the rafter and run the rope through it and back down to the floor. Since this second pulley is fixed, the mechanical advantage will remain the same.

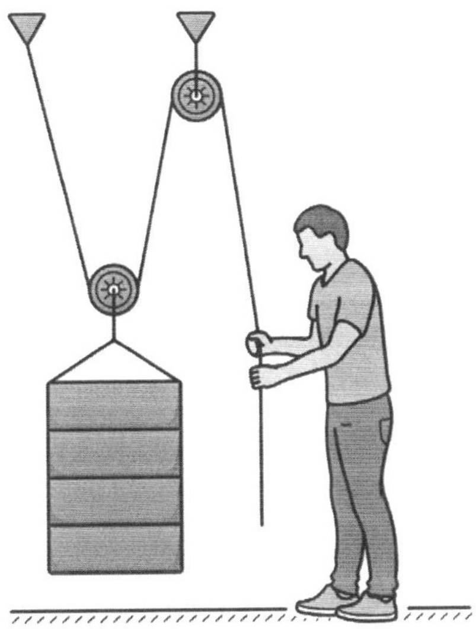

INCLINED PLANE

The inclined plane is perhaps the most common of the simple machines. It is simply a flat surface that elevates as you move from one end to the other. Consider how much easier it is for a person to walk up a long ramp than to climb a shorter but steeper flight of stairs; this is because the force required is diminished as the distance increases. Indeed, the longer the ramp, the easier it is to ascend.

Inclined planes often used to move heavy objects. For instance, moving a heavy box onto the back of a truck requires less force when pushing it up a ramp than when lifting it directly onto the truck bed. The longer the ramp, the greater the mechanical advantage, and the easier it will be to move the box. The mechanical advantage of an inclined plane is equal to the slant length divided by the rise of the plane.

$$\textbf{Mechanical Advantage} = \frac{\textbf{slant length}}{\textbf{rise}}$$

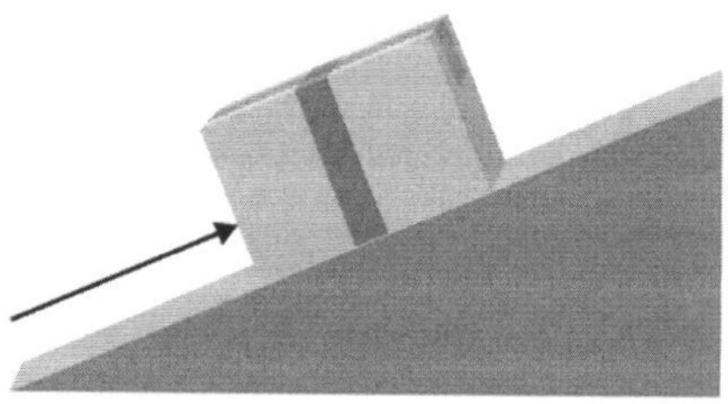

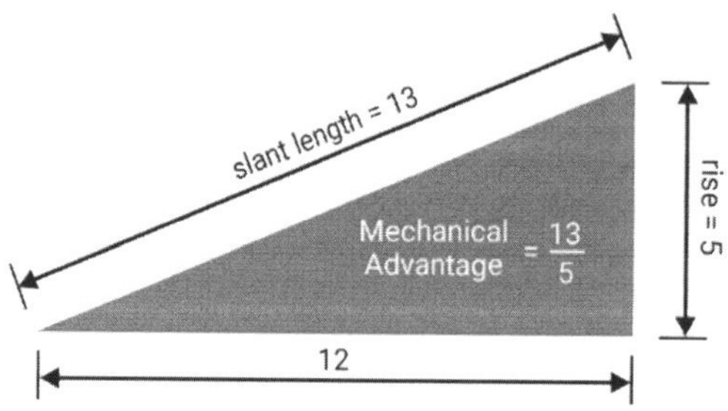

Screw

A screw is simply an inclined plane that has been wound around a cylinder so that it forms a sort of spiral.

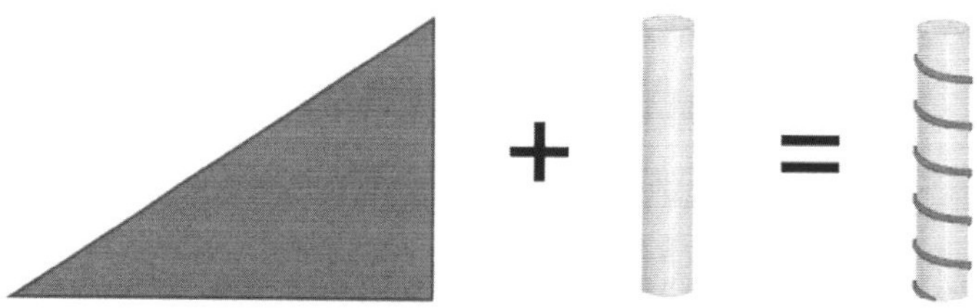

When it is placed into some medium, as for instance wood, the screw will move either forward or backward when it is rotated. The principle of the screw is used in a number of different objects, from jar lids to flashlights. The equation for the mechanical advantage is a modification of the inclined plane's equation. Because the rise of the inclined plane is the length along a screw, length between rotations is the rise. The slant length is equal the circumference of one rotation ($2\pi r$).

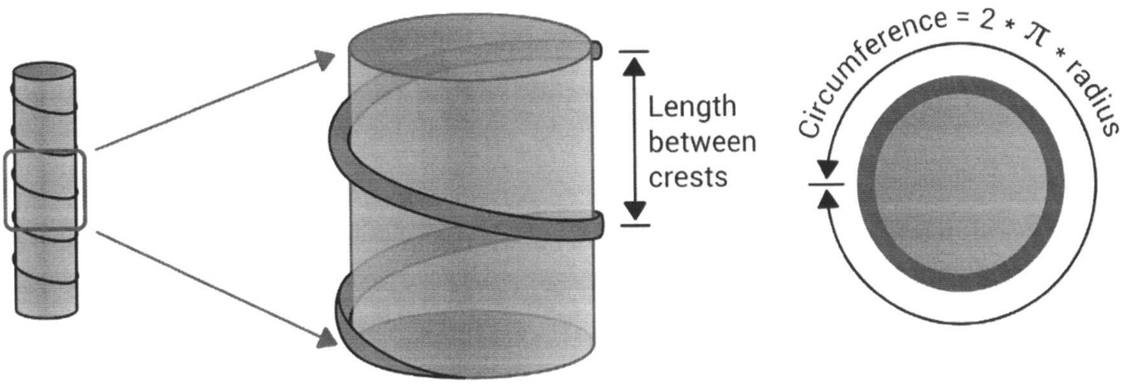

$$\textbf{Mechanical Advantage} = \frac{\textbf{2} \times \pi \times \textbf{radius}}{\textbf{length between crests}}$$

Wedge

A wedge is a variation on the inclined plane, in which the wedge moves between objects or parts and forces them apart. The unique characteristic of a wedge is that, unlike an inclined plane, it is designed to move. Perhaps the most familiar use of the wedge is in splitting wood. A wedge is driven into the wood by hitting the flat back end. The thin end of a wedge is easier to drive into the wood since it has less surface area and, therefore, transmits more force per area. As the wedge is driven in, the increased width helps to split the wood.

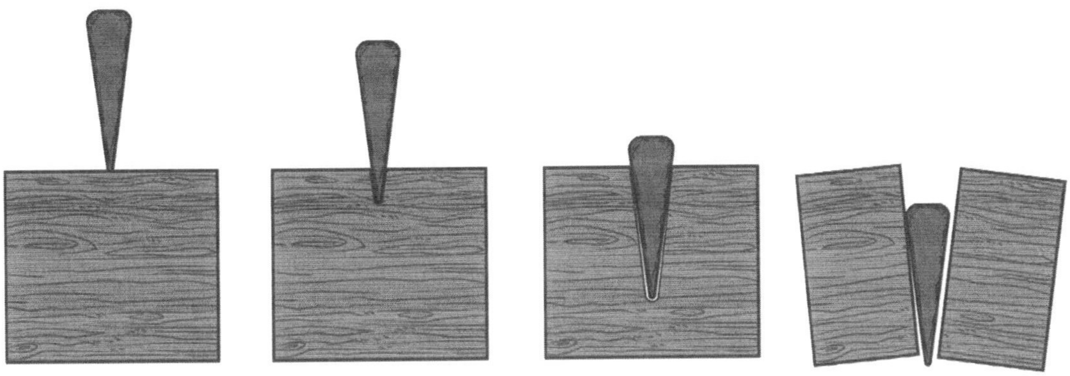

The longer and thinner the wedge, the greater the mechanical advantage. The equation for mechanical advantage of a wedge is:

$$\textbf{Mechanical Advantage} = \frac{\textbf{length}}{\textbf{width}}$$

Gears

Gears are a system of interlocking wheels that can create immense mechanical advantages. The amount of mechanical advantage, however, will depend on the gear ratio; that is, on the relation in size between the gears.

When a small gear is driving a big gear, the speed of the big gear is relatively slow; when a big gear is driving a small gear, the speed of the small gear is relatively fast.

The equation for the mechanical advantage is:

$$\textbf{Mechanical Advantage} = \frac{\text{torque}_{output}}{\text{torque}_{input}} = \frac{r_{output}}{r_{input}} = \frac{\#\text{ of teeth}_{output}}{\#\text{ of teeth}_{input}}$$

Note that mechanical advantage is greater than 1 when the output gear is larger. In these cases, the output velocity (ω) will be lower. The equation for the relative speed of a gear system is:

$$\frac{\omega_{input}}{\omega_{output}} = \frac{r_{output}}{r_{input}}$$

$$\textit{Mechanical Advantage} = \frac{\textit{teeth output}}{\textit{teeth input}} = \frac{20}{10} = 2$$

$$\textit{Mechanical Advantage} = \frac{\textit{teeth output}}{\textit{teeth input}} = \frac{16}{8} = 2$$

Gear Ratios

A gear ratio is a measure of how much the speed and torque are changing in a gear system. It is the ratio of output speed to input speed. Because the number of teeth is directly proportional to the speed in meshing gears, a gear ratio can also be calculated using the number of teeth on the gears. When the driving gear has 30 teeth and the driven gear has 10 teeth, the gear ratio is 3:1.

$$\text{Gear Ratio} = \frac{\#\text{ of teeth}_{driving}}{\#\text{ of teeth}_{driven}} = \frac{30}{10} = \frac{3}{1} = 3:1$$

This means that the smaller, driven gear rotates 3 times for every 1 rotation of the driving gear.

Uses of Gears

Gears are used to change the direction, location, and amount of output torque, as well as change the angular velocity of output.

Change output direction

Change torque location

Change torque amount

Change output velocity

Cams

In the study of motion, a final application often tested is the cam. A cam and follower system allows mechanical systems to have timed, specified, and repeating motion. Although cams come in varied forms, tests focus on rotary cams. In engines, a cam shaft coordinates the valves for intake and exhaust. Cams are often used to convert rotational motion into repeating linear motion.

Cams rotate around one point. The follower sits on the edge of the cam and moves along with the edge. To understand simple cams, count the number of bumps on the cam. Each bump will cause the follower to move outwards.

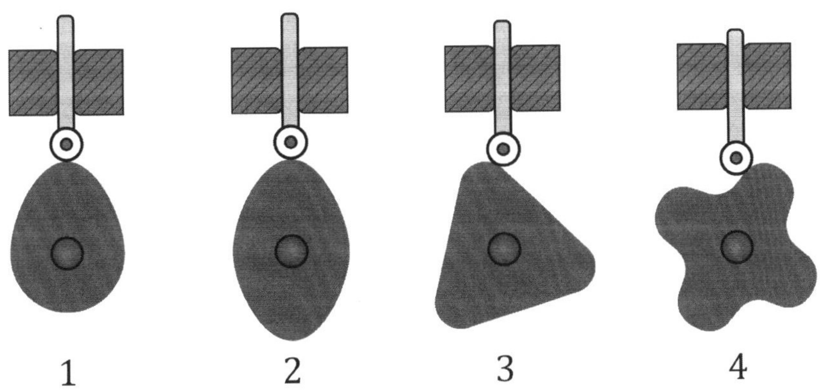

Another way to consider cams is to unravel the cam profile into a straight object. The follower will then follow the top of the profile.

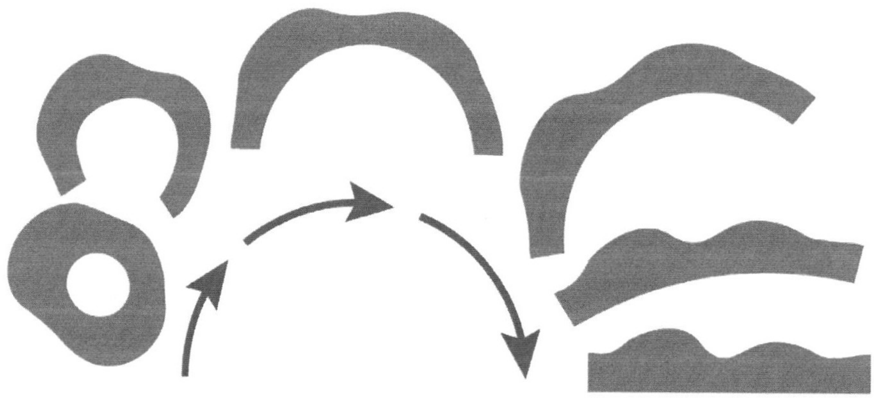

ENERGY

Energy is a word that has developed several different meanings in the English language, but in physics, it refers to the measure of a body's ability to do work. In physics, energy may not have a million meanings, but it does have many forms. Each of these forms, such as chemical, electric, and nuclear, is the capability of an object to perform work. However, the most commonly used concepts are mechanical energy and mechanical work. **Mechanical energy** is the sum of an object's kinetic and potential energies. While kinetic energy is linked to an object's motion, potential energy can be in a few different forms. The common forms of potential energy are gravitational and elastic.

KINETIC ENERGY

The **kinetic energy of an object** is that quality of its motion that can be related in a qualitative way to the amount of work performed on the object. Kinetic energy can be defined as $KE = \frac{mv^2}{2}$, in which m is the mass of an object and v is the magnitude of its velocity. Kinetic energy cannot be negative, since it depends on the square of velocity. Units for kinetic energy are the same as those for work: joules. Kinetic energy is a scalar quantity.

Changes in kinetic energy occur when a force does work on an object, such that the speed of the object is altered. This change in kinetic energy is equal to the amount of work that is done, and can be expressed as $W = KE_f - KE_i = \Delta KE$. This equation is commonly referred to as the work-kinetic energy theorem. If there are several different forces acting on the object, then W in this equation is the total work done by all the forces, or by the net force. This equation can be very helpful in solving some problems that would otherwise rely solely on Newton's laws of motion.

POTENTIAL ENERGY

Potential energy is the amount of energy that can be ascribed to a body or bodies based on configuration. There are a couple of different kinds of potential energy. **Gravitational potential energy** is the energy associated with the separation of bodies that are attracted to one another gravitationally. Any time you lift an object, you are increasing its gravitational potential energy. Gravitational potential energy can be found by the equation $PE = mgh$, where m is the mass of an object, g is the gravitational acceleration, and h is its height above a reference point, most often the ground.

Another kind of potential energy is **elastic potential energy**; elastic potential energy is associated with the compression or expansion of an elastic, or spring-like, object. Physicists will often refer to potential energy as being stored within a body, the implication being that it could emerge in the future.

Review Video: Potential and Kinetic Energy
Visit mometrix.com/academy and enter code: 491502

Elastic Potential Energy

Elastic potential energy is the potential for a certain amount of work to be done by one object on another using elastic compression or tension. The most common example is the spring. A spring will resist any compression or tension away from its equilibrium position (natural position). A small buggy is pressed into a large spring. The spring contains a large amount of elastic potential energy. If the buggy and spring are released, the spring will exert a force on the buggy, pushing it for a distance. This work will put kinetic energy into the buggy. The energy can be imagined as a liquid poured from one container into another. The spring pours its elastic energy into the buggy, which receives the energy as kinetic energy.

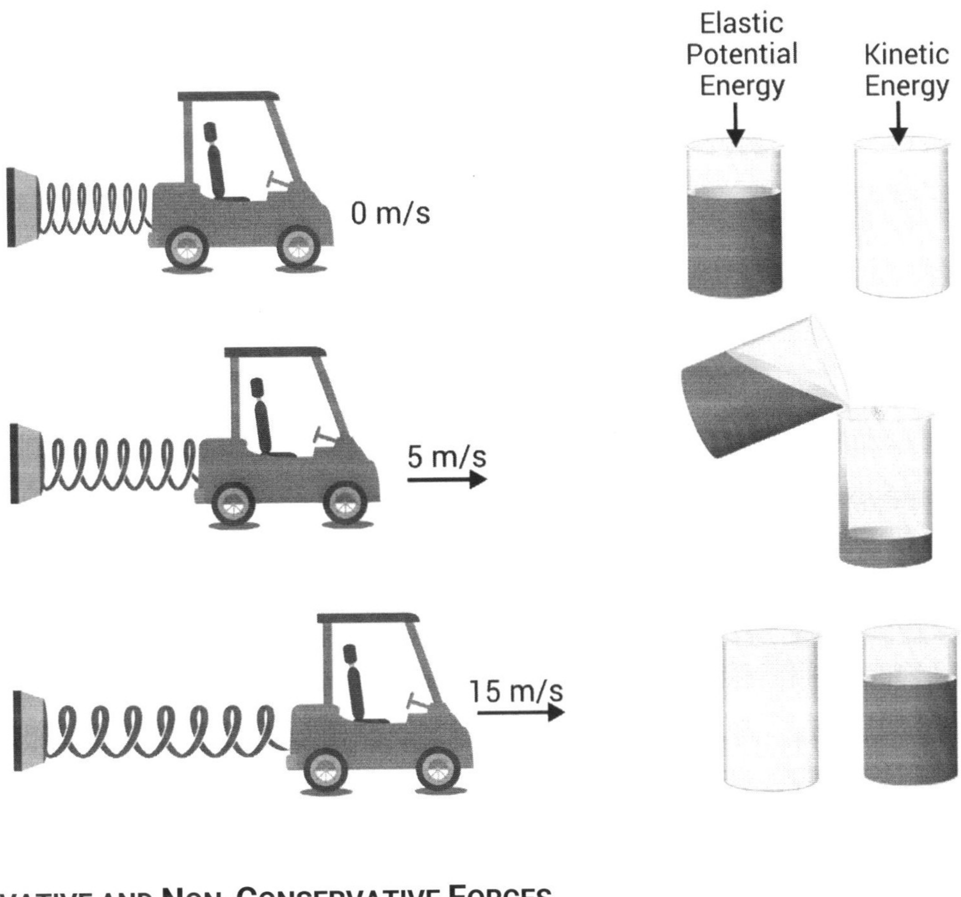

Conservative and Non-Conservative Forces

Forces that change the state of a system by changing kinetic energy into potential energy, or vice versa, are called **conservative forces**. This name arises because these forces conserve the total amount of kinetic and potential energy. Every other kind of force is considered non-conservative. One example of a conservative force is gravity. Consider the path of a ball thrown straight up into the air. Since the ball has the same amount of kinetic energy when it is thrown as it does when it returns to its original location (known as completing a closed path), gravity can be said to be a conservative force. More generally, a force can be said to be conservative if the work it does on an object through a closed path is zero. Frictional force would not meet this standard, of course, because it is only capable of performing negative work.

For example, imagine a ball moving perpendicular to the surface of the Earth, in other words straight up and down, with its weight being the only force acting on it. As the ball rises, the weight will be doing work on the ball, decreasing its speed and its kinetic energy and slowing it down until it momentarily stops. During this ascent, the potential energy of the ball will be rising. Once the ball begins to fall back down, it will lose potential energy as it gains kinetic energy. Mechanical energy is conserved throughout; the potential energy of the ball at its highest point is equal to the kinetic energy of the ball at its lowest point, just before to impact.

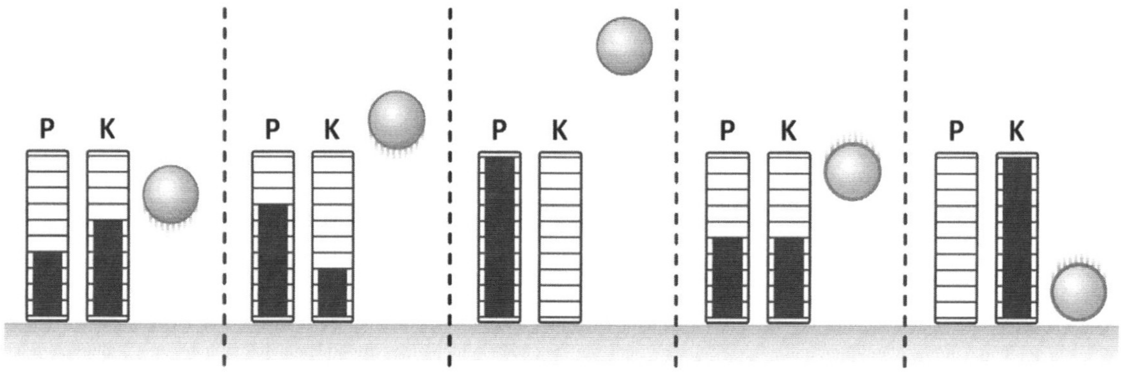

In systems where friction and air resistance are not negligible, we observe a different sort of result. For example, imagine a block sliding across the floor until it comes to a stop due to friction. Unlike a compressed spring or a ball flung into the air, there is no way for this block to regain its energy with a return trip. Therefore, we cannot say that the lost kinetic energy is being stored as potential energy. Instead, it has been dissipated and cannot be recovered. The total mechanical energy of the block-floor system has been not conserved in this case but rather reduced. The total energy of the system has not decreased, since the kinetic energy has been converted into thermal energy, but that energy is no longer useful for work.

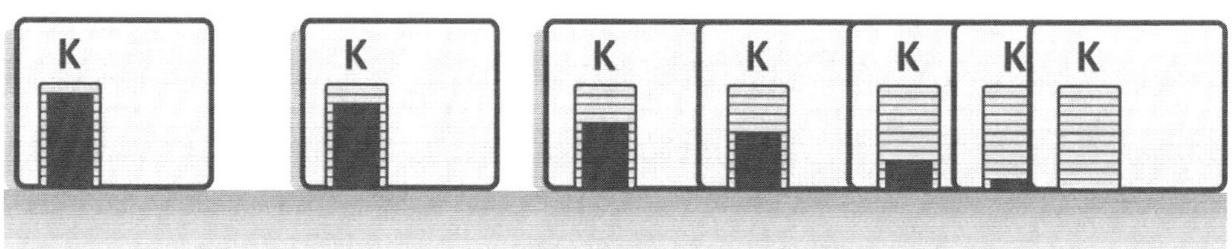

One-Dimensional Analysis of Work Done By a Variable Force

If the force on an object varies across the distance the object is moved, then a simple product will not yield the work. If we consider the work performed by a variable force in one dimension, then we are assuming that the directions of the force and the displacement are the same. The magnitude of the force will depend on the position of the particle. In order to calculate the amount of work performed by a variable force over a given distance, we should first divide the total displacement into a number of intervals, each with a width of Δx. We may then say that the amount of work performed during any one interval is $\Delta W = \boldsymbol{F}_{avg}\Delta x$, where $\boldsymbol{F}_{avg}$ is the average force over the interval Δx. We can then say that the total amount of work performed is the sum of all work performed during the various intervals. By reducing the interval to an infinitesimal length, we obtain the integral:

$$W = \int_{x_1}^{x_2} \boldsymbol{F}_x dx$$

This integral requires that the force be a known function of x.

Work Performed by a Spring

If we move a block attached to a spring from point x_i to point x_f, we are doing work on the block, and the spring is also doing work on the block. To determine the work done by the spring on the block, we can substitute $\boldsymbol{F}$ from Hooke's law into our equation for work performed by a variable force, and arrive at this measure: $W = \frac{k(x_i{}^2 - x_f{}^2)}{2}$. This work will be positive if $x_i{}^2 > x_f{}^2$, and negative if the opposite is true. If $x_i = 0$ and we decide to call the final position x, then we may change our equation: $W = \frac{-kx^2}{2}$. It is important to keep in mind that this is the work done by the spring. The work done by the force that moves the block to its final position will be a positive quantity.

Like all simple harmonic oscillators, springs operate by **storing and releasing potential energy**. The amount of energy being stored or released by a spring is equal to the magnitude of the work done by the spring during that same operation. The total potential energy stored in a spring can be calculated as $PE = \frac{kx^2}{2}$. Neglecting the effects of friction and drag, an object oscillating on a spring will continue to do so indefinitely, since total mechanical energy (kinetic and potential) is conserved. In such a situation, the period of oscillation can be calculated as $T = 2\pi \times \sqrt{\frac{m}{k}}$.

Displacement, Velocity, and Acceleration

Displacement

When something changes its location from one place to another, it is said to have undergone **displacement**. If we can determine the original and final position of the object, then we can determine the total displacement with the equation $\Delta \boldsymbol{x} = x_f - x_i$, where x_f is the final position and x_i is the initial position.

If the object has moved in the positive direction, then the final position will be greater than the original position, so we can say that the change was positive. If the final position is less than the original, however, displacement will be negative. Displacement along a straight line is an example of a vector quantity; it has both a magnitude and a direction. If an object travels from position $x = -5$ cm to $x = 5$ cm, it has undergone a displacement of 10 cm. If it traverses the same path in the opposite direction, its displacement is –10 cm. A vector that spans the object's displacement in the direction of travel is known as a displacement vector, with units of length.

Review Video: Displacement in Physics
Visit mometrix.com/academy and enter code: 236197

Determining Position

In order to determine anything about the motion of an object, we must first locate it. In other words, we must be able to describe its position relative to some reference point, often called an

origin. If we consider the origin as the zero point of an axis, then positive values correspond to the location of an object one direction, and negative values are locations in the exact opposite direction. If a particle is located 5 cm from the origin in the positive direction of the x-axis, its location is said to be $x = 5$ cm. If another particle is 5 cm from the origin in the negative direction of the x-axis, its position is $x = -5$ cm. These two particles are 10 cm apart. A vector whose starting point is the origin and whose endpoint is the location of an object is that object's position vector, with units of length.

VELOCITY

DIFFERENCE BETWEEN SPEED AND VELOCITY

Often, people confuse the words *speed* and *velocity*. There is a significant difference. The average velocity is based on the amount of displacement, a vector. Alternately, the average speed is based on the distance covered or the path length. The equation for speed is:

$$\textbf{average speed} = \frac{\textbf{total distance traveled}}{\textbf{change in time}}$$

Notice that we used total distance and *not* change in position, because speed is path-dependent.

If the plane traveling between cities had needed to fly around a storm on its way, making the distance traveled 50 miles greater than the distance the car traveled, the plane would still have the same total displacement as the car.

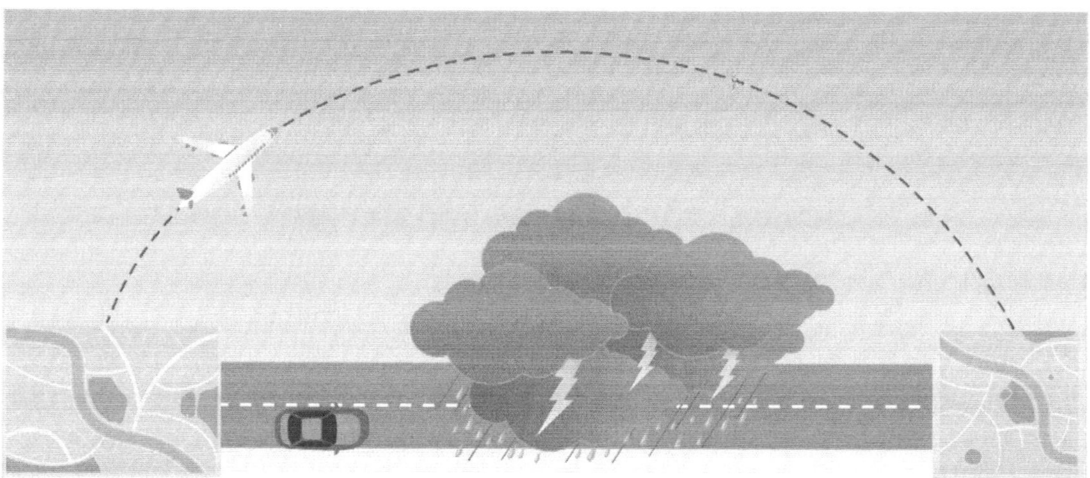

For this reason, the average speed can be calculated:

$$\text{plane average speed} = \frac{150 \text{ miles}}{1 \text{ hour}} = 150 \text{ miles per hour}$$

$$\text{car average speed} = \frac{100 \text{ miles}}{2 \text{ hours}} = 50 \text{ miles per hour}$$

INSTANTANEOUS VELOCITY

There are two types of velocity that are commonly considered in physics: average velocity and instantaneous velocity. In order to obtain the **instantaneous velocity** of an object, we must find its average velocity and then try to decrease Δt as close as possible to zero. As Δt decreases, it approaches what is known as a limiting value, bringing the average velocity very close to the instantaneous velocity. Instantaneous velocity is most easily discussed in the context of calculus-based physics.

Average Velocity

If we want to calculate the **average velocity** of an object, we must know two things. First, we must know its **displacement**, or the distance it has covered relative to a starting point. Second, we must know the **time it took to cover this distance**. Once we have this information, the formula for average velocity is: $\boldsymbol{v}_{avg} = \frac{(x_f - x_i)}{(t_f - t_i)}$, where the subscripts i and f denote the initial and final values of the position and time. In other words, the average velocity is equal to the change in position divided by the change in time. This calculation will indicate the average distance that was covered per unit of time. Average velocity is a vector and will always point in the same direction as the displacement vector (since time is a scalar and always positive).

Acceleration

Acceleration is the **change in the velocity** of an object. Like velocity, acceleration may be computed as an average or an instantaneous quantity. To calculate average acceleration, we may use the equation $\boldsymbol{a}_{avg} = \frac{v_f - v_i}{t_f - t_i}$, where the subscripts i and f denote the initial and final values of the velocity and time. The so-called instantaneous acceleration of an object can be found by reducing the time component to the limiting value until instantaneous velocity is approached. Acceleration will be expressed in units of distance divided by time squared; for instance, meters per second squared. Like position and velocity, acceleration is a vector quantity and will therefore have both magnitude and direction.

Review Video: Velocity and Acceleration
Visit mometrix.com/academy and enter code: 671849

Kinematics

Kinematic Equations

The phenomenon of constant acceleration allows physicists to construct a number of helpful equations. Perhaps the most fundamental equation of an object's motion is the **position equation**:

$$x_f = x_i + \boldsymbol{v}_i t + \frac{1}{2}\boldsymbol{a}t^2$$

If the object is starting from rest at the origin, this equation reduces to $x_f = \frac{at^2}{2}$. The position equation can be rearranged to give the **displacement equation**:

$$\Delta \boldsymbol{x} = \boldsymbol{v}_i t + \frac{1}{2}\boldsymbol{a}t^2$$

If the object's acceleration is unknown, the position or displacement may be found by the equation:

$$\Delta \boldsymbol{x} = \frac{(\boldsymbol{v}_f + \boldsymbol{v}_i)t}{2}$$

If the position of an object is unknown, the velocity may be found by the equation:

$$\boldsymbol{v}_f = \boldsymbol{v}_i + \boldsymbol{a}t$$

Similarly, if the time is unknown, the velocity after a given displacement may be found by the equation:

$$v_f = \sqrt{(v_i{}^2 + 2a\Delta x)}$$

CONCEPT OF PROJECTILE MOTION

When we discuss **projectile motion**, we are referring to the movement of an object through two dimensions during a free fall. Two-dimensional motion may be described using the same equations as one-dimensional motion, but two equations must be considered simultaneously. For basic equations for projectile motion, it is often assumed that the rate of gravitational acceleration on the Earth is $\boldsymbol{g} = 9.8\ \text{m/s}^2$, and that the effect of air resistance can be ignored (Note: take care with the sign on gravitational acceleration make sure that it always points toward the Earth). If a projectile is launched under such ideal conditions, we may say that its initial velocity is $\boldsymbol{v}_0 = v_0 \cos\theta\, \mathbf{i} + v_0 \sin\theta\, \mathbf{j}$. These two velocity components are sometimes written as $\boldsymbol{v}_{0x}$ and $\boldsymbol{v}_{0y}$, respectively.

PROJECTILE MOTION EXAMPLE

Simple projectile motion occurs when an object is in the air and experiencing only the force of gravity. We will disregard drag for this topic. Some common examples of projectile motion are thrown balls, flying bullets, and falling rocks. The characteristics of projectile motion are:

1. The horizontal component of velocity doesn't change
2. The vertical acceleration due to gravity affects the vertical component of velocity

Because gravity only acts downwards, objects in projectile motion only experience acceleration in the y-direction (vertical). The horizontal component of the object's velocity does not change in flight. This means that if a rock is thrown out off a cliff, the horizontal velocity (think of the shadow if the sun is directly overhead) will not change until the ball hits the ground.

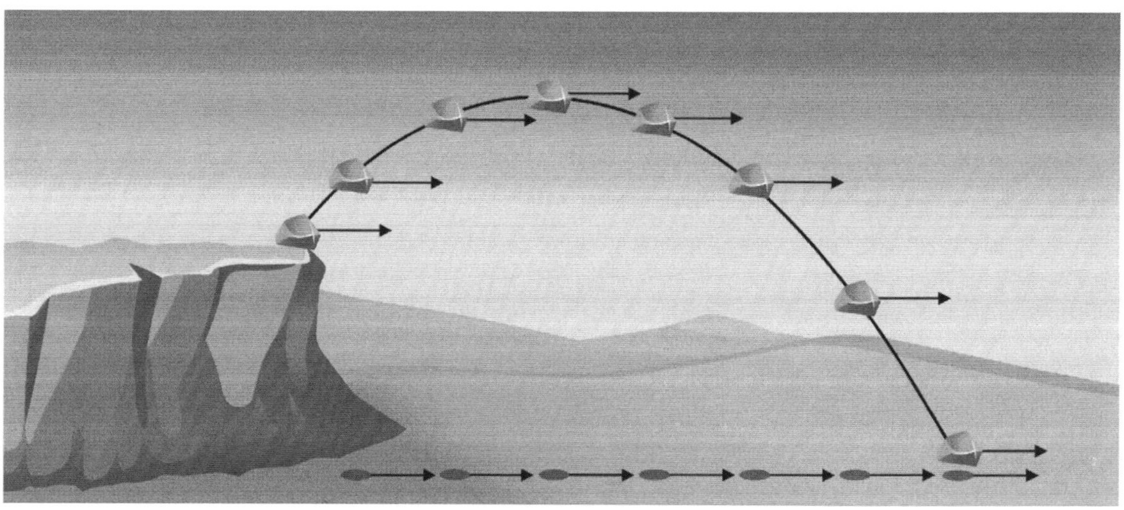

The velocity in the vertical direction is affected by gravity. Gravity imposes an acceleration of $g = 9.8\frac{\text{m}}{\text{s}^2}$ or $32\frac{\text{ft}}{\text{s}^2}$ downward on projectiles. The vertical component of velocity at any point is equal to:

$$\textbf{vertical velocity} = \textbf{original vertical velocity} - \textbf{g} \times \textbf{time}$$

When these characteristics are combined, there are three points of particular interest in a projectile's flight. At the beginning of a flight, the object has a horizontal component and a vertical component giving it a large speed. At the top of a projectile's flight, the vertical velocity equals zero, making the top the slowest part of travel. When the object passes the same height as the launch, the vertical velocity is opposite of the initial vertical velocity, making the speed equal to the initial speed.

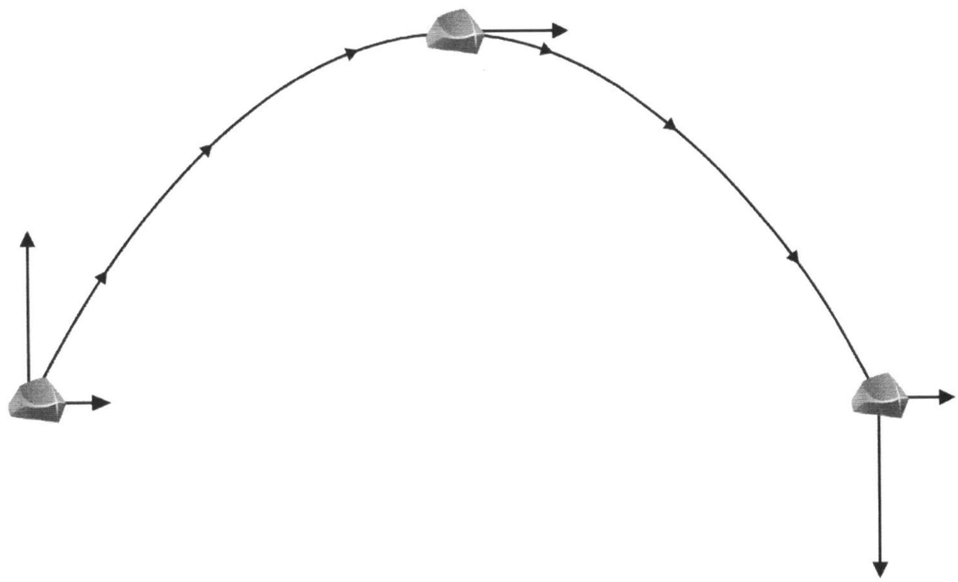

If the object continues falling below the initial height from which it was launched (e.g., it was launched from the edge of a cliff), it will have an even greater velocity than it did initially from that point until it hits the ground.

Review Video: Projectile Motion
Visit mometrix.com/academy and enter code: 719700

Example: If a cannon located at a height of 5 m above ground level fires a cannonball 250 m/s at an angle of $\frac{\pi}{6}$ from the horizontal, how far will the cannonball travel before hitting the ground?

When the cannonball hits the ground, it has been displaced by -5 m in the y-direction. Solving for the components of initial velocity yields $\boldsymbol{v}_{0x} = 216.5$ m/s and $\boldsymbol{v}_{0y} = 125$ m/s. Setting up the y-direction displacement equation results in the following: $-5 = 125t_f - 4.9t_f{}^2$. Solving for t_f yields an impact time of around 25.5 seconds. To find the horizontal distance covered, set up the displacement equation for the x-direction: $\Delta\boldsymbol{x} = \boldsymbol{v}_{0x}t_f + \frac{1}{2}\boldsymbol{a}_x\left(t_f\right)^2$. Since we ignore the effects of air resistance, acceleration in the x-direction is zero, yielding a flight distance of 5,530 m.

Uniform Circular Motion

We may say that a particle is in **uniform circular motion** when it is traveling in a circle, or circular arc, and at a constant speed. Crucially, we must note that such a particle is accelerating, even though the magnitude of its velocity does not change. This is because velocity is a vector, and consequently, any change in its direction is an acceleration. So, if we take two points on an arc of radius, r, separated by an angle, θ, and want to determine the time it will take a particle to move between these two points at a constant speed, $|\boldsymbol{v}|$, we can use the equation: $\Delta t = \frac{r\theta}{|\boldsymbol{v}|}$. The quantity $\frac{|\boldsymbol{v}|}{r}$ is often written as $\boldsymbol{\omega}$, or angular velocity, having units of radians per second, so the time may also be computed as $\Delta t = \frac{\theta}{\omega}$. The speed, or absolute value of the velocity, of an object in uniform circular motion is also called the tangential speed, because the object is always moving in a direction tangent to the circle. Similarly, an increase in the magnitude of this velocity is called **tangential acceleration**.

A very important component of uniform motion is the centripetal acceleration. This is the acceleration that changes the direction of the velocity vector to follow the circular arc. It is directed toward the center of the circle or arc and is described by $\boldsymbol{a}_c = \frac{|\boldsymbol{v}|^2}{r} = r\boldsymbol{\omega}^2$.

Relative Motion and Inertial Reference Frames

When we describe motion as being **relative**, we mean that it can only be measured in relation to something else. If a moving object is considered as it relates to some stationary object or arbitrary location, it will have a different measured velocity than it would if it were compared to some other object that is itself in motion. In other words, the measure of an object's velocity depends entirely on the reference frame from which the measurement is taken. When performing measurements of this kind, we may use any reference point we like. However, once we have decided on a reference point, we must be consistent in using it as the basis for all of our measurements, or else we will go astray. Additionally, if we want to be able to apply Newton's laws of motion or Galilean principles of relativity, we must select an **inertial reference frame**: that is, a reference frame that is not accelerating or rotating. A car traveling at a constant speed in a straight line is an inertial reference frame. A car moving in uniform circular motion is not.

An object's velocity with respect to a frame fixed to the Earth can be computed by measuring its velocity from any inertial reference frame and combining that velocity by vector addition with the velocity of the inertial frame with respect to the Earth. For instance, if a man is traveling in the x-direction at 20 m/s, and he throws a rock out the window at a relative velocity of 15 m/s in the y-direction, the rock's velocity with respect to the Earth is found by adding the two vectors:

$$\boldsymbol{v}_r = 20\mathbf{i} + 15\mathbf{j} \text{ m/s}$$

Laws of Motion

Newton's Laws

Newton's First Law

Before Newton formulated his laws of mechanics, it was generally assumed that some force had to act on an object continuously in order to make the object move at a **constant velocity**. Newton, however, determined that unless some other force acted on the object (most notably friction or air resistance), it would continue in the direction it was pushed at the same velocity forever.

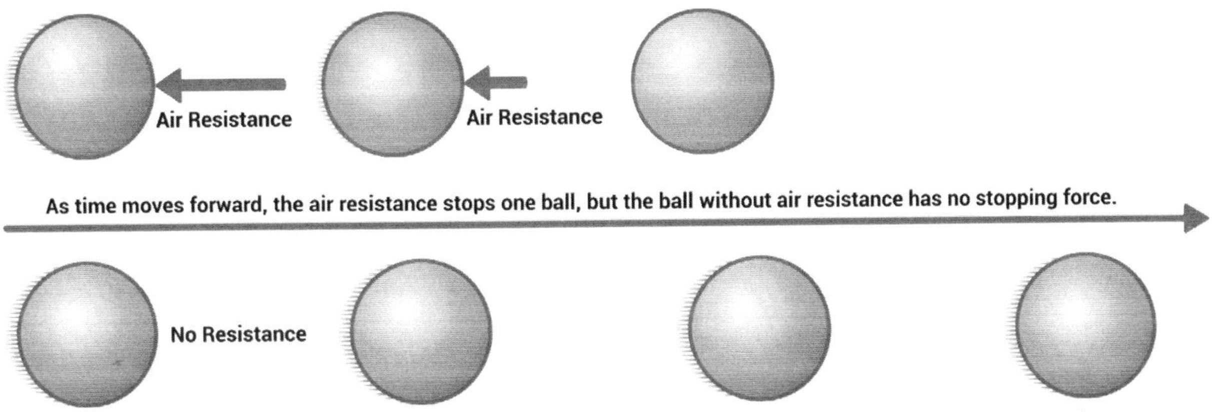

In this light, a body at rest and a body in motion are not all that different, and Newton's first law makes little distinction. It states that a body at rest will tend to remain at rest, while a body in motion will tend to remain in motion. This tendency of a body to remain in its present state of motion is referred to as **inertia**. In order for the body's state of motion to change, it must be acted on by a non-zero net force. **Net force** is the vector sum of all forces acting on a body. If this vector sum is zero, then there is no unbalanced force, and the body will remain in its present state of motion. It is important to remember that this law only holds in inertial reference frames.

Review Video: Newton's First Law of Motion
Visit mometrix.com/academy and enter code: 590367

Newton's Second Law

Newton's second law states that an **object's acceleration** is directly proportional to the net force acting on the object, and inversely proportional to the object's mass. It is generally written in equation form $\boldsymbol{F} = m\boldsymbol{a}$, where $\boldsymbol{F}$ is the net force acting on a body, m is the mass of the body, and $\boldsymbol{a}$ is its acceleration. It is important to note from this equation that since the mass is always a positive quantity, the acceleration vector is always pointed in the same direction as the net force vector. Of course, in order to apply this equation correctly, one must clearly identify the body to which it is being applied. Once this is done, we may say that $\boldsymbol{F}$ is the vector sum of all forces acting on that body, or the net force. This measure includes only those forces that are external to the body; any internal forces, in which one part of the body exerts force on another, are discounted.

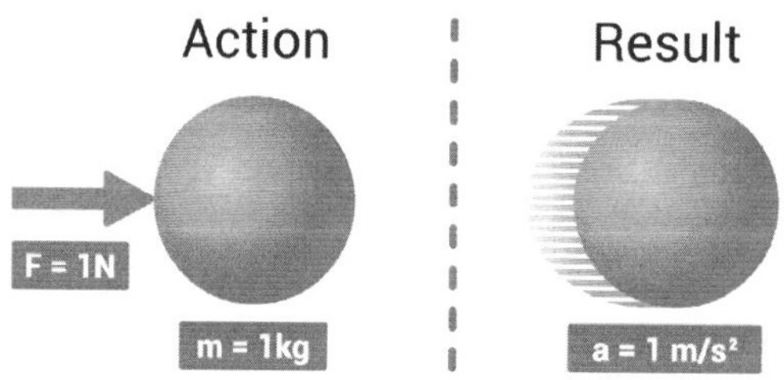

Newton's second law somewhat encapsulates his first, because it includes the principle that if no net force is acting on a body, the body will not accelerate. As was the case with his first law, Newton's second law may only be applied in inertial reference frames.

> **Review Video: Newton's Second Law of Motion**
> Visit mometrix.com/academy and enter code: 737975

NEWTON'S THIRD LAW

Newton's third law of motion can be stated as: **for every force, there is an equal and opposite force**. When a hammer strikes a nail, the nail hits the hammer just as hard. If we consider two objects, A and B, then we may express any contact between these two bodies with the equation $\boldsymbol{F}_{AB} = -\boldsymbol{F}_{BA}$. It is important to note in this kind of equation that the order of the subscripts denotes which body is exerting the force. Although the two forces are often referred to as the **action** and **reaction** forces, in physics there is really no such thing. There is no implication of cause and effect in the equation for Newton's third law. At first glance, this law might seem to forbid any movement at all. We must remember, however, that these equal, opposite forces are exerted on different bodies with different masses, so they will not cancel each other out.

As an example, consider two spring-based scales, both tipped on their sides, with the weighing surfaces facing each other. If scale #1 is pressing scale #2 into the wall, it exerts a force on scale #2, measurable by the reading on scale #2. However, because scale #1 is exerting a force on scale #2, scale #2 is exerting a force on scale #1 with an opposite direction, but the same magnitude.

> **Review Video: Newton's Third Law of Motion**
> Visit mometrix.com/academy and enter code: 838401

Equilibrium and Friction

NORMAL FORCE

The word *normal* is used in mathematics to mean perpendicular, and so the force known as normal force should be remembered as the perpendicular force exerted on an object that is resting on some other surface. For instance, if a box is resting on a horizontal surface, we may say that the normal force is directed upwards through the box (the opposite, downward force is the weight of the box). If the box is resting on a wedge, the normal force from the wedge is not vertical but is perpendicular to the surface.

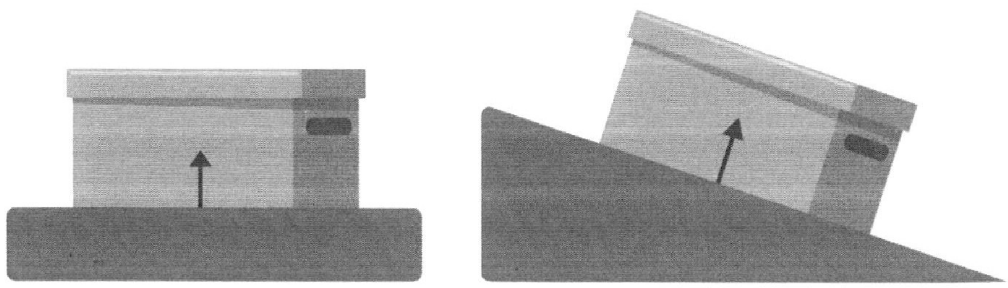

STATIC AND KINETIC FRICTIONAL FORCES

In order to illustrate the concept of friction, let us imagine a book resting on a table. As it sits there, the force of its weight (W) is equal and opposite to the normal force (N). If, however, we were to exert a force (F) on the book, attempting to push it to one side, a frictional force (f) would arise, equal and opposite to our force. This kind of frictional force is known as **static frictional force**.

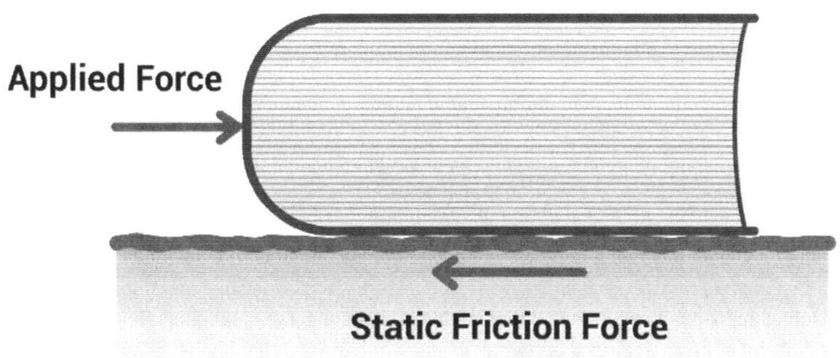

As we increase our force on the book, however, we will eventually cause it to accelerate in the direction of our force. At this point, the frictional force opposing us will be known as **kinetic frictional force**.

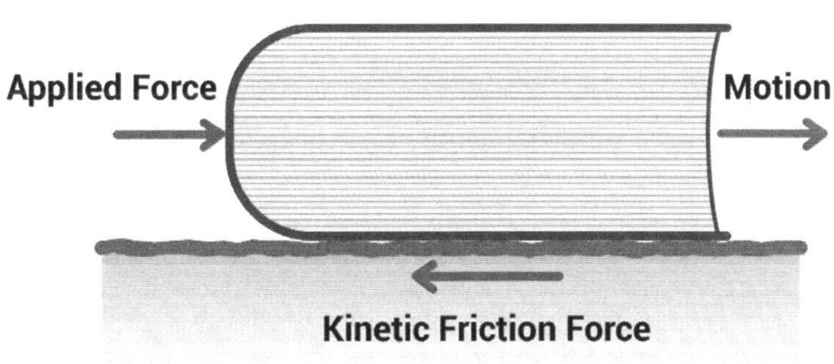

For the most part, kinetic frictional force is lower than static frictional force, and so the amount of force needed to maintain the movement of the book will be less than that needed to initiate movement. For wheels and spherical objects on a surface, static friction at the point of contact allows them to roll, but there is a frictional force that resists the rolling motion as well, due primarily to deformation effects in the rolling material. This is known as rolling friction, and tends to be much smaller than either static or kinetic friction.

Coefficient of Friction

If an object does not move when a horizontal force $\boldsymbol{F}$ is applied, then the **static frictional force** $(\boldsymbol{f}_s)$ is exactly equal and opposite to $\boldsymbol{F}$, i.e., $\boldsymbol{f}_s = -\boldsymbol{F}$. Static frictional force has a maximum value, however, which is expressed as $\boldsymbol{f}_{s,max} = \mu_s N$, in which μ_s is the coefficient of static friction, and N is the magnitude of the normal force. If the magnitude of horizontal force applied to an object exceeds the maximum value of static friction, the object will begin to move. Once the object has begun to slide, the frictional force will generally decrease. The value to which the frictional force will diminish is expressed as $\boldsymbol{f}_k = \mu_k N$, in which μ_k is the coefficient of kinetic friction. For objects inclined to roll, such as balls or wheels, there is a rolling frictional force that resists the continued rolling of such an object. This force is expressed by $\boldsymbol{f}_r = \mu_r N$, in which μ_r is the coefficient of rolling friction. All of these frictional coefficients are dimensionless. Since the value of the frictional force depends on the interaction of the body and the surface, it is usually described as friction between the two.

Review Video: Friction
Visit mometrix.com/academy and enter code: 716782

Equilibrium

We may say that an object is in a **state of equilibrium** when it has a **constant linear momentum** $(\boldsymbol{p})$ at its center of mass, or when **angular momentum** $(\boldsymbol{L})$ **is also constant about the center of mass**. In other words, a wheel may be in equilibrium when it is spinning at a constant speed, and a hockey puck may be in equilibrium as it slides across ice. These are both examples of **dynamic equilibrium**. The phrase **static equilibrium**, however, is reserved for objects in which both linear and angular momentum are at zero. An object sitting on a table could be considered as being in static equilibrium.

Balanced Forces

An object is in equilibrium when the sum of all forces acting on the object is zero. When the forces on an object sum to zero, the object does not accelerate. Equilibrium can be obtained when forces in the y-direction sum to zero, forces in the x-direction sum to zero, or forces in both directions sum to zero.

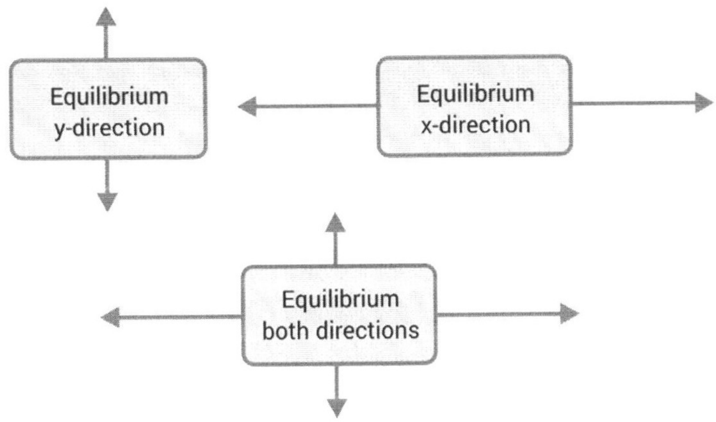

In most cases, a problem will provide one or more forces acting on an object and ask for a force to balance the system. The force will be the opposite of the current force or sum of current forces.

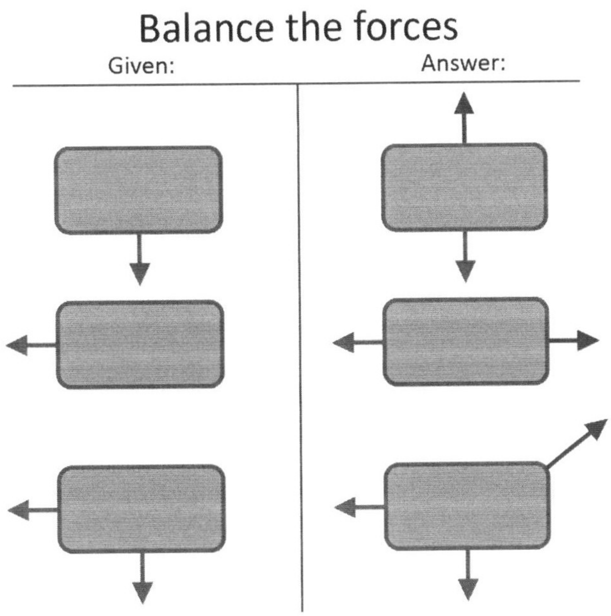

Using Equilibrium Conditions

For a **body in equilibrium**, the net force vector and the net torque vector will both be equal to zero. For the most common cases, two-dimensional systems, these conditions can be fully expressed by one or two force summation equations and one torque summation equation. Torque summations may be taken about any point on the body, though strategic placement can make calculations simpler. To determine the **torque exerted by a force**, multiply the magnitude of the force by the perpendicular distance to the point of interest. It will be necessary to decide in advance which direction of torque (clockwise or counterclockwise) will be considered positive.

For example, if we have a bar of known mass, m, that is suspended by cables at each end and whose center of mass is two thirds of the way along its length, L, we can use the equilibrium conditions to determine the tension in each cable. Gravity exerts a force of $-mg$ on the bar's center of mass.

Translational equilibrium conditions tell us that $\boldsymbol{T}_1 + \boldsymbol{T}_2 - m\boldsymbol{g} = 0$. Setting the total torque about the center of mass equal to zero, considering counterclockwise torque to be positive, yields the equation $\boldsymbol{T}_2\left(\frac{L}{3}\right) - \boldsymbol{T}_1\left(\frac{2L}{3}\right) = 0$. Solving these equations results in $\boldsymbol{T}_1 = \frac{m\boldsymbol{g}}{3}$ and $\boldsymbol{T}_2 = \frac{2m\boldsymbol{g}}{3}$. This result makes sense since the center of mass is closer to the second cable.

Translational and Rotational Equilibrium

If a body is in **translational equilibrium**, then its linear momentum will be constant, and there will be a net force of zero. Likewise, a body in rotational equilibrium will have a constant angular momentum, and again there will be a net torque of zero. Both of these equations are vector equations, and as such are both equivalent to three scalar equations for the three dimensions of motion, though in most instances, only one or two dimensions will be considered at a time. We may say that the two requirements for a body to be in equilibrium are that the vector sum of all the external forces acting on the body must be zero, and the vector sum of all the external torques acting on the body must also be zero. Conversely, if we are told that a body is in equilibrium, we may assume that both of these conditions will hold, and that we can use them to find unknown forces or torques.

Conservation of Energy and Momentum

Applying Conservation of Rotational Energy and Angular Momentum

A metal hoop of mass m and radius r is released from rest at the top of a hill of height h. Assuming that it rolls without sliding and does not lose energy to friction or drag, what will be the hoop's angular and linear velocities upon reaching the bottom of the hill?

The hoop's initial energy is all potential energy, $PE = mgh$. As the hoop rolls down, all of its energy is converted to **translational** and **rotational kinetic energy**. Thus, $mgh = \frac{1}{2}m\boldsymbol{v}^2 + \frac{1}{2}I\boldsymbol{\omega}^2$. Since the moment for a hoop is $I = mr^2$, and $\boldsymbol{\omega} = \frac{v}{r}$, the equation becomes $mgh = \frac{1}{2}m\boldsymbol{v}^2 + \frac{1}{2}mr^2\left(\frac{\boldsymbol{v}^2}{r^2}\right)$, which further simplifies to $gh = \boldsymbol{v}^2$. Thus, the resulting velocity of the hoop is $\boldsymbol{v}_f = \sqrt{gh}$, with an angular velocity of $\boldsymbol{\omega}_f = \frac{\boldsymbol{v}_f}{r}$. Note that if you were to forget about the energy converted to rotational motion, you would calculate a final velocity of $\boldsymbol{v}_f = \sqrt{2gh}$, which is the **impact velocity** of an object dropped from height h.

Angular momentum, $\boldsymbol{L}$, of an object is defined as its moment of inertia multiplied by its angular velocity, or $\boldsymbol{L} = I\boldsymbol{\omega}$. Consider a planet orbiting the sun with an elliptical orbit where the small radius is r_S and large radius is r_L. Find the angular velocity of the planet when it is at distance r_S from the sun if its velocity at r_L is $\boldsymbol{\omega}_L$.

Since the size of a planet is almost insignificant compared to the interplanetary distances, the planet may be treated as a single particle of mass m, giving it a moment about the sun of $I = mr^2$. Since the gravitational force is incapable of exerting a net torque on an object, we can assume that the planet's angular momentum about the sun is a constant, $\boldsymbol{L}_L = \boldsymbol{L}_S$. Thus, $m{r_L}^2\boldsymbol{\omega}_L = m{r_S}^2\boldsymbol{\omega}_S$. Solving this equation for $\boldsymbol{\omega}_S$ yields $\boldsymbol{\omega}_S = \boldsymbol{\omega}_L\left(\frac{r_L}{r_S}\right)^2$.

Mass-Energy Relationship

Because mass consists of atoms, which are themselves formed of subatomic particles, there is an energy inherent in the composition of all mass. In other words, it would require a significant input of energy to form all the atoms in a given mass from their most basic particles. This rest energy is the energy that Einstein refers to in his famous mass-energy relation $E = mc^2$, where c is the speed of light in a vacuum. In theory, if all the particles in a given mass were converted directly to energy (e.g., by matter-antimatter annihilation), it would give off energy $E = mc^2$. For example, if this were to happen to a single gram of mass, the resulting outburst of energy would be $E = 9 \times 10^{13}$ J, enough energy to provide power for over 2,000 average households for a whole year.

In some nuclear reactions, small amounts of mass are converted to energy. The amount of energy released can be calculated through the same relation, $E = mc^2$. Most such reactions involve mass losses on the order of 10^{-30} kg.

Weight and Mass

Weight

Not to be confused with mass (quantity of matter), weight the term for the force due to the gravitational attraction between the masses of the two bodies. This force is described by the expression $\frac{Gm_1m_2}{r^2}$, where G is the gravitational constant, m_1 and m_2 are the masses of the two objects, and r is the distance between the centers of mass. Since the majority of humans are concerned with events close to the surface of the Earth, one of the masses (M_E) and the distance (R_E) are essentially constant and are combined into $\boldsymbol{g}$, which is the acceleration due to gravity near the surface of the Earth $\left(\boldsymbol{g} = \frac{GM_E}{(R_E)^2}\right)$. Thus, we can express weight as $\boldsymbol{W} = m\boldsymbol{g}$. Since it is a force, the SI unit for weight is the Newton. As a vector, $\boldsymbol{W}$ can be expressed as either $-mg\mathbf{j}$ or $-W\mathbf{j}$, in which $\mathbf{j}$ is the direction on the axis pointing away from the Earth.

Review Video: Mass, Weight, Volume, Density, and Specific Gravity
Visit mometrix.com/academy and enter code: 920570

Electrical Properties of Materials

Common Means of Transferring Electrical Charge

Charge is transferred in three common ways: conduction, induction, and friction. **Conduction**, as the name implies, takes place between conductive materials. There must be a point of contact between the two materials and a potential difference, such as when a battery is connected to a circuit. **Induction also requires conductive materials. It occurs when a conductive material encounters a changing magnetic field**. The change can be the result of a changing magnetic field or the material moving within a constant magnetic field. Charge transfer due to **friction** does not require conductive materials. When two materials are rubbed together, electrons may be transferred from one to the other, leaving the two materials with equal and opposite charges. This is observed when shoes are dragged across a carpeted floor.

Review Video: Charging by Conduction
Visit mometrix.com/academy and enter code: 502661

Conductors, Insulators, and Semiconductors

In many materials, electrons are able to move freely; these are known as **conductors**. Due to their atomic structure and delocalized electrons, **metals** tend to be the best conductors, particularly copper and silver. Highly conductive wires are instrumental in creating low-resistance pathways for electrons to travel along within a circuit.

Other materials naturally inhibit the movement of charge and are known as **insulators**. Their electrons are tightly held by the individual constituent atoms. Glass, pure water, wood, and plastic are all insulators. Insulators are necessary in circuits to prevent charge from escaping to undesirable places, such as an operator's hand. For this reason, most highly conductive materials are covered by insulators.

Semiconductors, as the name suggests, are materials that only partially conduct electrical charge. The elements silicon and germanium are both common semiconductors, and are frequently used in microelectronic devices because they allow for tight control of the rate of conduction. In many cases, the conduction ability of semiconductors can be controlled by adjusting the temperature of the material.

Doping Semiconductors

Resistivity is the physical property of resistance of different materials: metals, which easily conduct electricity, have low resistivity; insulators have high resistivity; and the resistivity of **semiconductors** falls in between (example: silicon). **Doping** is the process of mixing different semiconductor atoms in order to control conductivity of the material. **N-type semiconductors** have an excess of electrons as a result of the doping process; when an electric field is applied, a negative pole forms due to the buildup of negatively charged electrons (example: silicon doped with antimony). **P-type semiconductors** have a shortage of electrons; when an electric field is applied, a positive pole forms (example: silicon doped with boron).

Introduction to Circuits and Current

Electric Current

Charge is a physical property of particles. For the particles of an atom, protons have a positive charge of +1, neutrons have no charge, and **electrons** have a negative charge of −1. Like charges repel each other (positive and positive or negative and negative), and opposite charges attract (negative and positive). The **net charge** of an atom or molecule can be found by adding up all the protons and electrons that it contains. When dealing with charge on the macro level, it is helpful to aggregate the charges in a material with different units. The coulomb is the SI unit for charge and is equivalent to about 6.24×10^{18} charged particles.

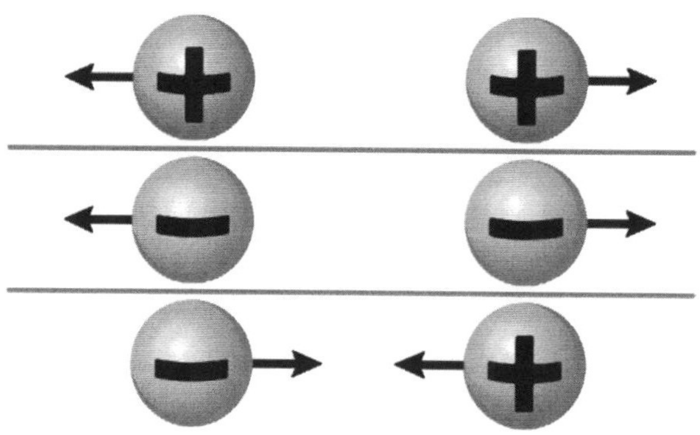

Electric current is the net rate of flow of charge (electrons) past a specific point, as in a wire or circuit. Current (represented by I in equations) is measured in amperes or amps (A). An ampere is equal to one coulomb per second $\left(\mathrm{A} = \frac{\mathrm{C}}{\mathrm{s}}\right)$. Ammeters are tools that can be used to measure current.

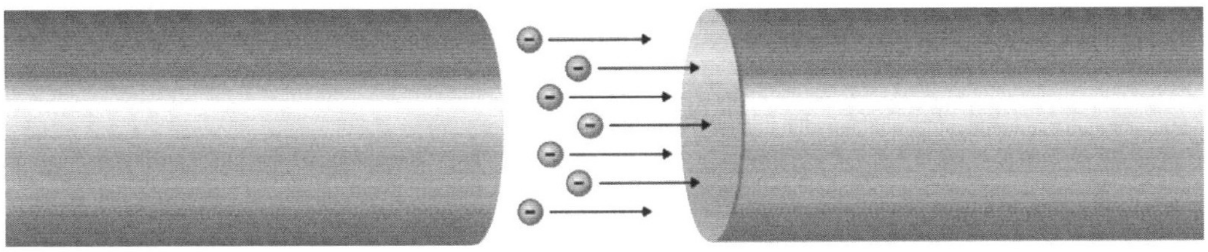

Electric current carries energy much like moving balls carry energy.

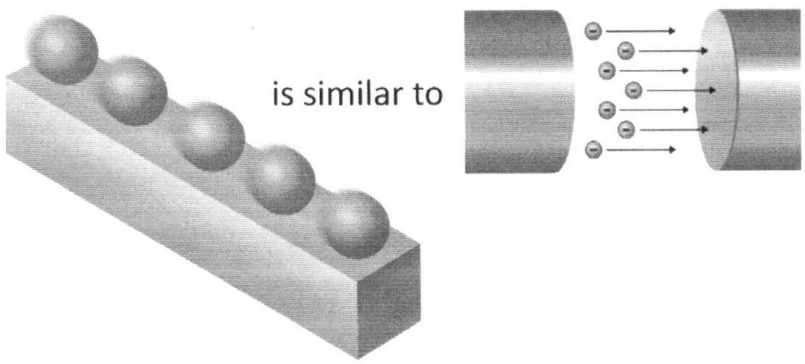

Electron flow theory states that electrons (e^-) flow from the negative terminal to the positive terminal. **Electricity** is the form of energy that exists statically (potential energy) with an accumulation of protons or electrons or dynamically with their movement (current).

Review Video: Electric Charge Visit mometrix.com/academy and enter code: 323587

Alternating and Direct Current

For circuits with **direct current** (DC), when current flows in only one direction, the voltage and current are constant. Direct current is supplied by batteries and is used in cell phones, ships, and planes. **Alternating current** (AC), in which current periodically reverses direction, can be produced using generators and is used for land-based applications (including in homes) because less power is lost when electricity travels long distances. In the United States, AC electricity is supplied most commonly at 120 V and 240 V.

Electric Potential

Electric potential energy is the energy stored in a charge by virtue of its proximity to other charged regions. It can be calculated in the same way as calculating the amount of work required to move it to that location from an infinite distance away. The work required to move a charge of magnitude q from infinity to a distance r from another charge of magnitude Q is calculated to be $PE_e = W = \frac{kQq}{r}$, where k is the **electrostatic constant**.

Electric potential, V, is closely related to electric potential energy. The potential due to a charge Q can be found by dividing the electric potential energy of another charge q by its magnitude, $V = \frac{PE_e}{q}$, or by the equation $V = \frac{kQ}{r}$.

The difference between the electric potential of two points is known as **voltage**. It is measured in volts, or joules per coulomb. Since it is impractical to find a point of zero absolute electric potential, for each system a reference point or ground is defined, to which all other points in the system may be related. Voltage is similar to gravitational potential energy.

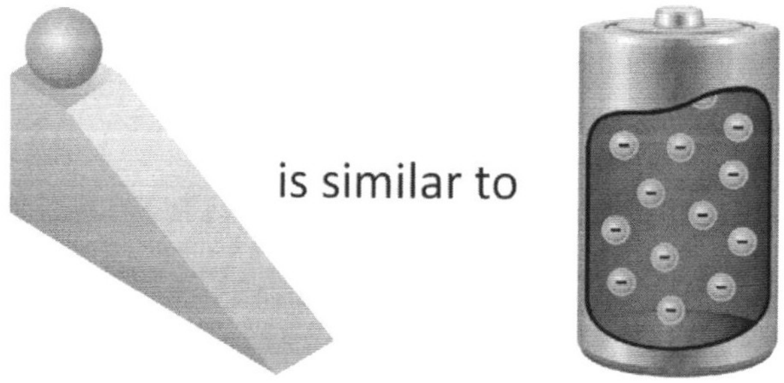

Electromotive Force and Common EMF Devices

A force that maintains a potential difference between two locations in a circuit is known as an **electromotive force (emf).** A device that creates this force is referred to as an **emf device**. The most common emf device is the battery. **Batteries** operate by converting chemical energy stored in the electrolyte, the internal chemical material, into electrical energy. The reaction causes a lack of electrons on the cathode, and when the circuit is connected, they flow from the anode, creating a flow of current. The electrolyte's composition also determines whether the battery is classified as acidic or alkaline, and wet or dry. Another emf device is the **photocell**, also commonly called the solar cell, since most photocells are powered by the sun. These operate by absorbing photons, which cause the electrons to be excited and flow in a current, a process of converting light energy into electrical energy. A third type of emf device is the **generator**. This device converts mechanical energy to electrical energy. A generator may be powered by such diverse sources as gasoline engines, flowing water, or even manually powered cranks. These devices utilize a rotating shaft to spin a coil within a magnetic field, creating a potential difference by induction.

Ohm's Law

If we were to apply the exact same potential difference between the ends of two geometrically similar rods, one made of copper and one made of glass, we would create vastly different currents. This is because these two substances have different **resistances. Ohm's Law** describes the relation between applied voltage and induced current, $V = IR$. This is one of the most important tools of circuit analysis. Resistance, then, can be calculated as $R = \frac{V}{I}$. The SI unit for resistance is the **ohm** (Ω), equal to a volt per ampere. When a component is placed into a circuit to provide a specific resistance, it is known as a **resistor**. For a given potential difference, the greater the resistance is to the current, the smaller the current will be. Electrical resistance is much like friction, resisting flow and dissipating energy.

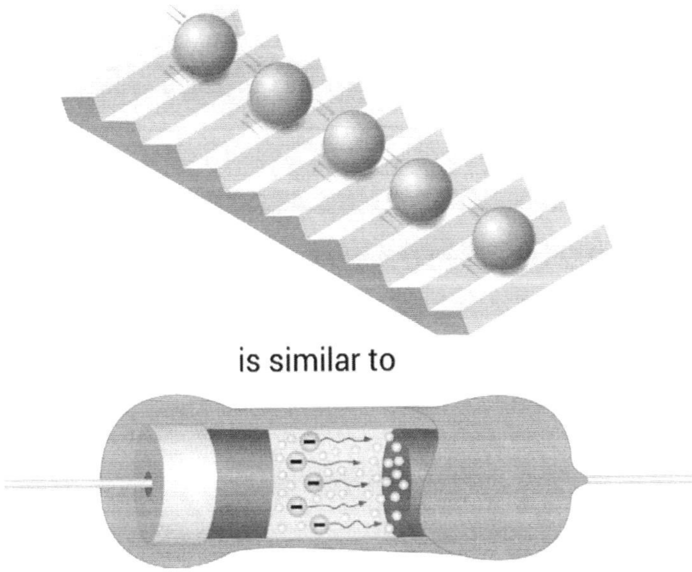

If we wish to look instead at the quality of the material of which the resistor is made, then we must consider resistivity. **Resistivity**, ρ, is a physical property of every material, which, if known, can be used to size a resistor for a specific resistance. Resistance is dictated by both the material and the dimensions of the resistor, given by the relation $R = \frac{\rho L}{A}$, where L is the effective length of the resistor and A is the effective cross-section. Alternatively, an unknown resistivity may be calculated by rearranging the equation as $\rho = \frac{RA}{L}$.

Resistivity will often change with temperature. In these cases, the relevant resistivity may be calculated $\rho = p_{ref}\left(1 + \alpha(T - T_{ref})\right)$, where α is the resistivity proportionality constant and T is the material temperature.

Review Video: Resistance of Electric Currents
Visit mometrix.com/academy and enter code: 668423

GROUND

Grounding is the process of neutralizing the charge of an object by removal of excess electrons to or donation of additional electrons by a much larger object (example: the Earth). This ground or large object can seemingly infinitely donate or accept electrons without mathematically significant changes to its net voltage. Examples of grounds include lighting rods and the round component of a three-pronged plug, as used for home appliances. Current does not usually flow through air, but lightning is the visible current that results when charge builds up in clouds; lightning rods provide a safe, low-resistance ground so the high-voltage current is less likely to be destructive. The round component of three-pronged plugs serves as one of the residential applications of this concept.

Energy and Power

Electric circuits operate by **transferring** electrical energy from one location in the circuit to another. Some devices in a circuit can store and release energy while other devices, like resistors, dissipate energy. **Power** is a measure of the rate at which energy is stored, released, transferred, or dissipated. It is measured in watts (W), or joules per second. Power is calculated by $P = VI$. The amount of power being released by a 9-V battery producing a current of 5 A is 45 W. When calculating the amount of power dissipated by a resistor, Ohm's Law can be combined with the power equation to form two other equations for power, $P = I^2R$ and $P = \frac{V^2}{R}$.

When power consumption over long periods of time needs to be measured, it will often be measured in units of kilowatt-hours, which is the amount of energy consumed at a rate of 1 kW over the course of an hour. One kilowatt-hour is equal to 3,600 kJ.

Capacitors and Dielectrics

Capacitors are devices used in circuits to store energy in the form of electric fields. They are most often composed of two oppositely charged parallel plates separated by a medium, generally air. This medium is referred to as the capacitor's **dielectric**.

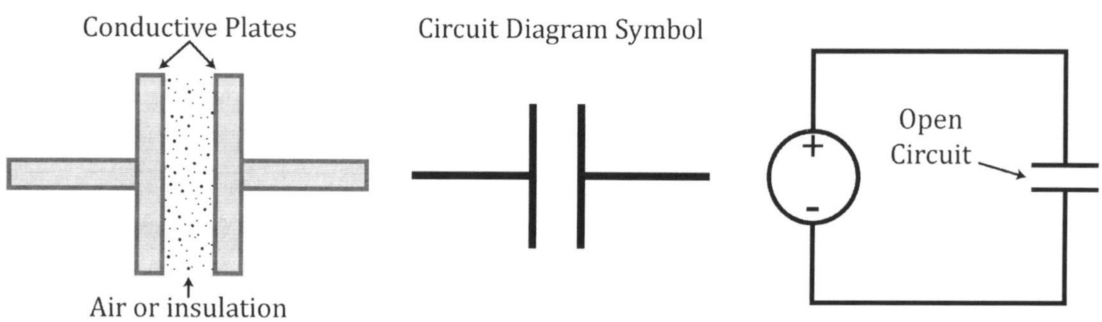

The dielectric material dictates the amount of energy in the electric field and, consequently, the amount of energy that can be stored by the capacitor. The measurable quality of a capacitor is known as its **capacitance**, which is defined as the amount of charge that it can store per volt of potential difference. This is given by the equation $C = \frac{Q}{V}$, with capacitance having units of farads or coulombs per volt. Physically, the capacitance depends on three things: the **area** of the parallel plates, the **separation distance** between them, and the **dielectric** material. For cases in which the separation distance is insignificant compared to the area, the capacitance can be found by the equation $C = \frac{\varepsilon A}{d}$, where ε is the permittivity of the dielectric material. Often, instead of being given the permittivity, we will be given the dielectric constant, κ, which is the ratio of the permittivities of the material and air, $\kappa = \frac{\varepsilon}{\varepsilon_{air}}$. This yields an obvious result of $\kappa_{air} = 1$.

The energy stored in a capacitor can be calculated in three different ways: $E = \frac{CV^2}{2} = \frac{Q^2}{2C} = \frac{VQ}{2}$. Another quantity associated with capacitors is the electric field energy density, η. This energy density is found by $\eta = \frac{\varepsilon E^2}{2}$.

Inductors

When current passes through a wire coil, a magnetic field develops. An **inductor** is an electrical component made of a coil of wire that can store energy and opposes the rate of change of alternating current flowing through it; however, direct current passes through easily. They can be used as filters, sensors, motors, and transformers.

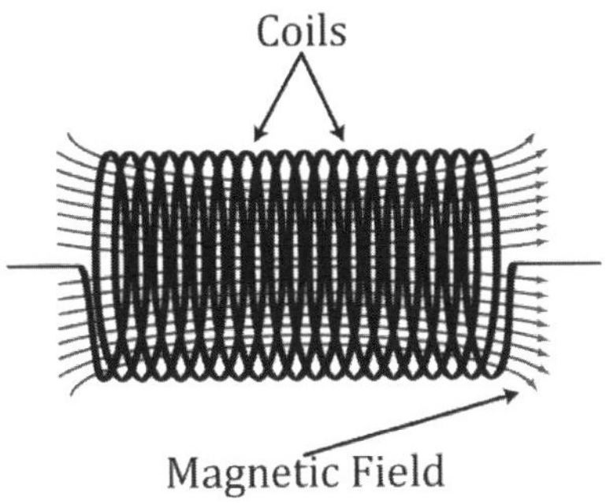

Circuit Diagram Symbol

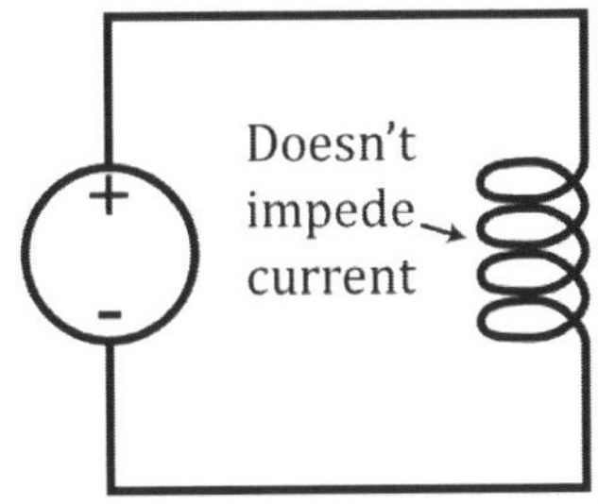

Inductance is the measure of ability of an inductor to resist changes in current. **Faraday's law of induction describes the ways voltage** or electromagnetic frequency can be generated by changing the magnetic environment in a coil of wire by moving a magnet within it, changing the external magnetic field of the magnet, or changing the area of the coil.

Capacitors and Inductors in AC Circuits

Capacitors and inductors both oppose immediate acceptance of the flow reversal of alternating current. This opposition is referred to as **impedance** and is similar to resistance, also having units of ohms, but unlike resistance, impedance is a complex value, meaning that it may have an **imaginary component** as well as a **real component**. For ideal capacitors and inductors, impedance is purely imaginary, and for ideal resistors, impedance is purely real. It is only when combining the effects of these devices that the full expression for impedance, Z, is necessary: $Z = R + X_i$, where $i = \sqrt{(-1)}$. X is a quantity known as reactance. For capacitors, $X_c = \frac{1}{\omega C}$, where ω is the angular frequency of the current, and for inductors, $X_L = \omega L$.

Other Electrical Components

Diodes

Diodes are a basic component of circuits, but they can't be described using Ohm's law; they operate as an electrical "valve", only allowing current to pass in one direction. This allows them to rectify alternating current by converting it to direct current, which is preferred or necessary for some applications. A common example is the light-emitting diode (LED) bulb, which emits light when powered more efficiently than regular light bulbs.

Circuit Diagram Symbol

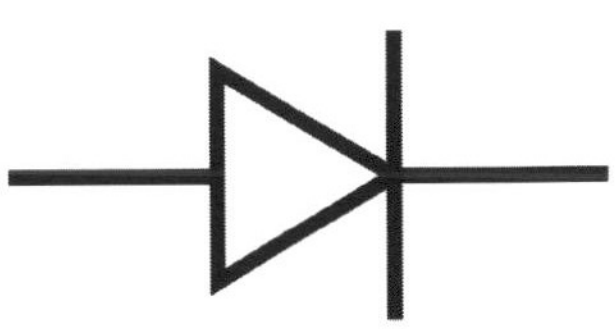

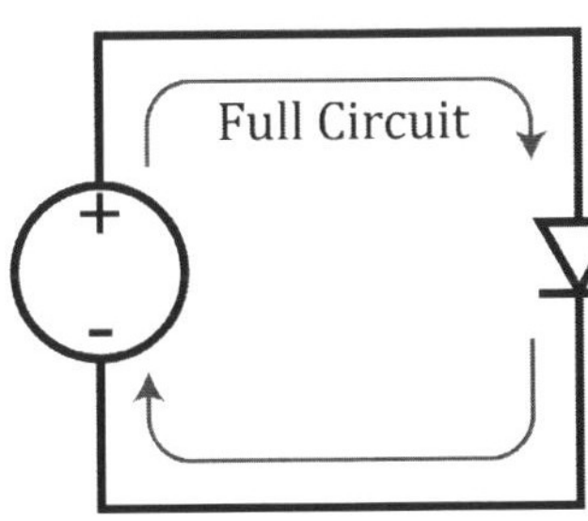

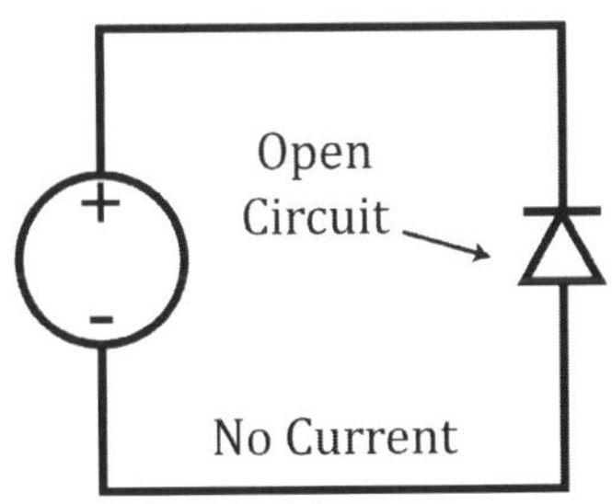

A p-n junction diode is formed by fusing a p-type semiconductor and an n-type semiconductor. It is considered a solid-state device because electricity flows through solid material rather than a vacuum tube. The p-region of the junction is positively charged and the n-region is negatively charged. Reverse bias occurs when the diode is connected such that the positive voltage is applied to the n-region; forward bias occurs when the positive voltage is applied to the p-region.

Transistors

A bipolar junction transistor, p-n-p or n-p-n, consists of two p-n junction diodes arranged back-to-back with three electrical leads or terminals: the emitter, the collector, and the base. Transistors are used to boost electrical signals or switch them on or off at high speeds. A large current flows from the emitter to the collector, and a smaller current entering through the base lead can be used to control the larger collector current.

Transformers

Transformers are devices made of two or more coils of wire that use induction to transfer electricity between circuits. A **step-up transformer**'s input (primary) voltage is lower than its output (secondary) voltage; and a **step-down transformer**'s input voltage is higher than its output voltage. This allows for electricity to be to be generated safely at a lower voltage (example: 12 kV), passed through a step-up transformer for transport through power lines at high voltage (example: 400 kV), and passed through step-down transformers for distribution and use (example: 240 V residential use).

Motors and Generators

Motors use electromagnetic induction to convert electrical energy (electricity) to mechanical energy (motion). In a **DC motor**, torque is produced by magnetic force, which results from current passing through coil located in a magnetic field. They have been around for more than 100 years and are simple, inexpensive, and easy to maintain. In **AC (synchronous) motors**, torque is produced the same way as in DC motors, but much higher current is required, and they are inefficient. **Induction (asynchronous) motors** are more common, and they rotate a magnetic field in order to induce alternating current.

Generators use electromagnetic induction to convert mechanical energy to electrical energy. **AC generators** mechanically turn a coil in a magnetic field to produce voltage output and induce alternating current.

Simple Circuits

The Use of Ohm's Law and Kirchhoff's Laws

Circuit analysis is the process of determining the **current** or **voltage drop** across devices of interest in a circuit. Ohm's Law is useful in doing this since it definitively relates the current to the voltage drop for resistors, $V = IR$. Kirchhoff's voltage law (KVL) states that if you sum the voltage drops across all devices in any closed loop of a circuit, the sum will always be zero, $V_1 + V_2 + \cdots + V_n = 0$. This law is particularly useful if there are multiple closed-loop pathways in a circuit. Kirchhoff's current law (KCL) states that the amount of current entering a point must equal the amount of current leaving, $I_{in} = I_{out}$. This law may also be expanded to apply to the current entering and leaving a larger region of a circuit. In any given circuit analysis, it may be necessary to use all three of these laws.

Another important principle to remember in an ideal circuit is that any two points connected by only wire are at equal voltage. Only devices on the circuit may change the voltage. In actual practice, however, all wire has some amount of resistance. A battery that provides an EMF of V_B is only able to deliver a voltage to the circuit of $V = V_B - IR_B$, where R_B is the internal resistance of the battery. To express this concept in an ideal circuit, we would need to add a small resistor in series after the battery.

Measuring Devices

There are several devices that allow various quantifiable properties of a circuit to be measured to a great degree of accuracy. An **ammeter** is a device placed in series with a circuit to measure the current through that location. Ideally, an ammeter has as little internal resistance as possible to prevent altering the current it is trying to measure. A **voltmeter** measures the voltage or potential difference between two locations in a circuit. It has two leads that are connected in parallel with the circuit and consists of a very high resistance and an ammeter in series. This allows only a very small amount of current to be diverted through the voltmeter, but enough to determine the voltage by Ohm's Law. A **galvanometer** is the primary working component of an ammeter. It operates based on the idea that a wire in a magnetic field will experience a force proportional to the amount of current it is carrying. It converts the observed current into a dial reading. A **potentiometer** is a variable resistor, often controlled by a knob, that allows an operator to control the amount of voltage or current provided to a given circuit. They are commonly used in volume-control knobs. Potentiometers can also be called voltage dividers. Their use in circuit measurement is for finding voltages by comparing them to known voltages. A **multimeter** is a device that combines the functions of all the above devices into one. In addition to voltage, current, resistance and capacitance, they can typically measure inductance, frequency, and other quantities.

Resistance in Series Circuits

A **series circuit** is a loop through which charge can flow along only one path. Resistance of resistors (labeled R_n) lined up in series is additive, so $R_{total} = R_1 + R_2 + R_3 + \cdots$ for all resistors in that series. Current (I) is consistent in all locations throughout a closed series circuit, so $I_{battery} = I_{R_1} = I_{R_2} = I_{R_3} = \cdots$, regardless of the number of elements in the series. Charge at the positive terminal of the battery experiences a **voltage drop** (ΔV), or loss of potential energy, as it passes through each resistor, such that its voltage will be zero at the negative terminal of the battery. Therefore, $\Delta V_{battery} = \Delta V_1 + \Delta V_2 + \Delta V_3 + \cdots$, where each ΔV_n represents the voltage drop across each resistor in series.

Problem Solving with Series Circuits

Using the labeled diagram of a series circuit, solve the following problems:

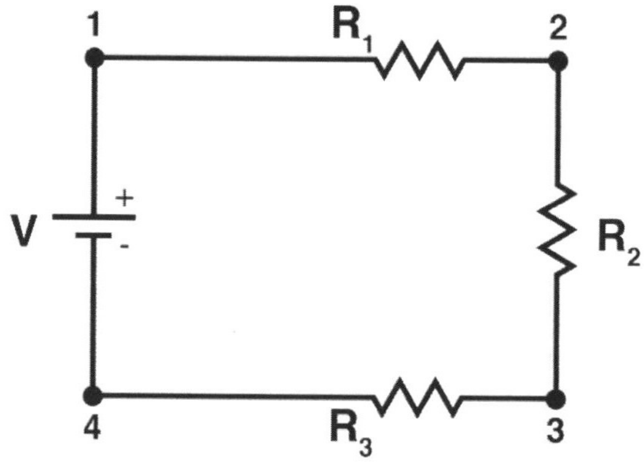

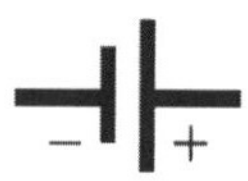

V = Voltage source (battery)

R = Resistor

Example 1: If each resistor is 3 Ω and the battery is 9 V, what is the current at each of the indicated corners?

Step 1:	Step 2:	Step 3:
Given: $R_1 = R_2 = R_3 = 3\ \Omega$ Equation: $R_{total} = R_1 + R_2 + R_3$ Solve: $R_{total} = 3\ \Omega + 3\ \Omega + 3\ \Omega = 9\ \Omega$	Given: $V_{battery} = 9$ V Equation: $I = \frac{V}{R}$ Solve: $I_{battery} = \frac{9\text{ V}}{9\ \Omega} = 1$ A	Because current is the same throughout the circuit, current at each corner is the same: $I_{total} = I_1 = I_2 = I_3 = I_4 = 1\ A$

Example 2: If the current at point 3 is 4 Amps, and each resistor is 1 Ω, what is the battery voltage?

Step 1:	Step 2:	Step 3:
Given: $I_3 = 4$ A The circuit is in series so current is the same throughout: $I_{total} = 4$ A	Given: $R_1 = R_2 = R_3 = 1\ \Omega$ Equation: $R_{total} = R_1 + R_2 + R_3$ Solve: $R_{total} = 1\ \Omega + 1\ \Omega + 1\ \Omega = 3\ \Omega$	Equation: $V_{total} = I_{total}(R_{total})$ Solve: $V_{total} = (4\text{ A})(3\ \Omega) = 12$ V

Resistance in Parallel Circuits

Parallel circuits provide multiple pathways for current to follow, which adjusts the way that current, voltage, and resistance interact when compared to series circuits. Because current (I) can follow multiple pathways, it is divided among those pathways at each branch, so $I_{total} = I_1 + I_2 + I_3 + \cdots$, where 1, 2, and 3 represent each unique branch. In this example, there are 3.

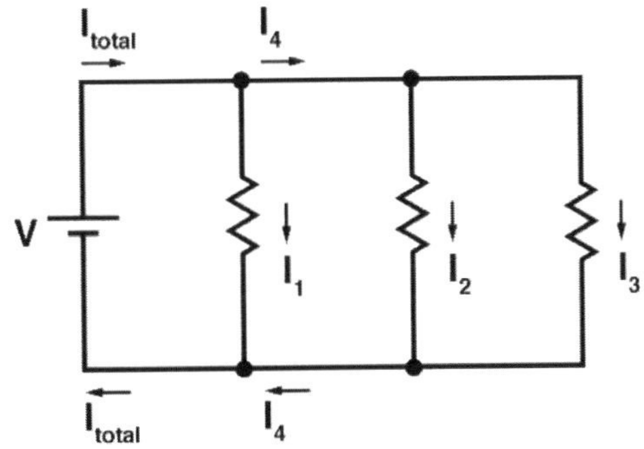

Equivalent resistance (R_{eq}) is the amount of resistance in a parallel circuit, represented as if there was only one resistor in series. All of the resistors in parallel can be simplified using the following equation:

$$\frac{1}{R_{eq}} = \frac{1}{R_1} + \frac{1}{R_2} + \frac{1}{R_3}$$

Because a charge will only pass through one resistor in the parallel circuit and not all three, the voltage drop across each resistor will be the same as that of the battery. Therefore, voltage drops for parallel circuits follow this rule:

$$\Delta V_{battery} = \Delta V_1 = \Delta V_2 = \Delta V_3 = \cdots$$

Note: If multiple resistors exist on a branch of a parallel circuit, they are in series and should be added together ($R_{total} = R_1 + R_2 + R_3 + \cdots$) before dealing with them as part of a parallel circuit.

Problem Solving with Parallel Circuits

Using the labeled diagram of a parallel circuit, solve the following problems:

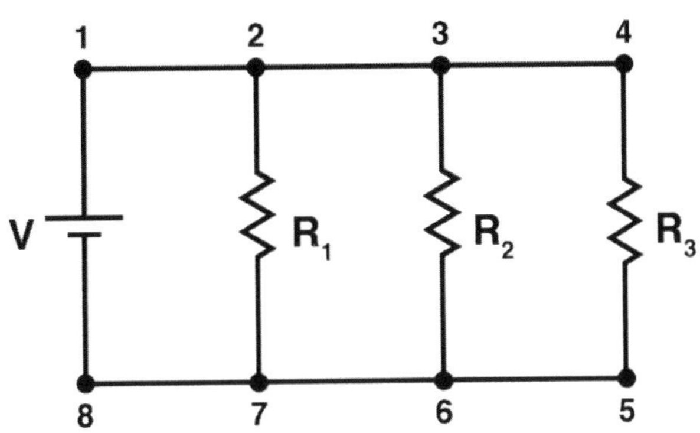

Example 1: If each resistor is 3 Ω and the battery is 9 V, what is the current at each of the indicated points (1-8) and each resistor?

Step 1:
Given: $R_1 = R_2 = R_3 = 3\ \Omega$
Equation: $\frac{1}{R_{eq}} = \frac{1}{R_1} + \frac{1}{R_2} + \frac{1}{R_3}$
Solve: $\frac{1}{R_{eq}} = \frac{1}{3\ \Omega} + \frac{1}{3\ \Omega} + \frac{1}{3\ \Omega}$

$$\frac{1}{R_{eq}} = \frac{3}{3\ \Omega}$$

$$R_{eq} = 1\ \Omega$$

Step 2:
Given: $V_{batt} = 9\text{ V}$
Equation: $I_{total} = \frac{V_{batt}}{R_{eq}}$
Solve: $I_{total} = \frac{9\text{ V}}{1\ \Omega} = 9\text{ A}$

Step 3:
Equation: $\Delta V_n = I_{R_n}(R_n)$
Solve: $I_{R_1} = \frac{9\text{ V}}{3\ \Omega} = 3\ A$
Current is the same for each branch in this example because $R_1 = R_2 = R_3 = 3\ \Omega$

Using this information and the additive properties of current in parallel circuits, the current through the following points and resistors is:

$$I_1 = I_2 = I_7 = I_8 = I_{total} = 9\text{ A}$$
$$I_3 = I_6 = 6\text{ A}$$
$$I_4 = I_5 = 3\text{ A}$$
$$I_{R_1} = I_{R_2} = I_{R_3} = 3\text{ A}$$

Example 2: If the current at point 4 is 4 Amps, and $R_1 = 3\ \Omega$; $R_2 = 2\ \Omega$; $R_3 = 6\ \Omega$, what is the total current?

Step 1:
Given: $R_3 = 6\ \Omega$; $I_4 = I_{R_3} = 4\ A$
Equation: $\Delta V_3 = I_{R_3}(R_3)$
Solve: $\Delta V_3 = (4\text{ A})(6\ \Omega) = 24\text{ V}$

Step 2:
Given: $R_1 = 3\ \Omega$; $R_2 = 2\ \Omega$
Equation: $I_n = \frac{V}{R_n}$
Solve: $I_1 = \frac{24\text{ V}}{3\ \Omega} = 8\text{ A}$

$$I_2 = \frac{24\text{ V}}{2\ \Omega} = 12\text{ A}$$

Step 3:
Equation: $I_{total} = I_1 + I_2 + I_3$
Solve: $I_{total} = 8\text{ A} + 12\text{ A} + 4\text{ A}$

$$I_{total} = 24\text{ A}$$

Capacitors and Inductors in Circuits

Capacitors have combination rules opposite to those of resistors. **Capacitors in series** have an equivalent value of:

$$C_{eq} = \left(\frac{1}{C_1} + \frac{1}{C_2} + \cdots + \frac{1}{C_n}\right)^{-1}$$

Capacitors in parallel have equivalence of:

$$C_{eq} = C_1 + C_2 + \cdots + C_n$$

Inductors follow the same combination rules as resistors. **Inductors in series** have an equivalent value of:

$$L_{eq} = L_1 + L_2 + \cdots + L_n$$

Inductors in parallel have equivalence of

$$L_{eq} = \left(\frac{1}{L_1} + \frac{1}{L_2} + \cdots + \frac{1}{L_n}\right)^{-1}$$

RC Circuits

An RC circuit consists of a battery wired in series with a **resistor** and a **capacitor**. Since a capacitor in steady state allows no current flow, it makes no sense to analyze a steady-state RC circuit. Instead, we will look at an RC circuit that has only just been connected, with the capacitor uncharged. The battery supplies voltage V_B to the circuit, and since the capacitor's voltage is initially zero, the voltage across the resistor is initially V_B, giving an initial current of $I = \frac{V_B}{R}$. As current flows, the charge on the capacitor increases, which in turn creates an opposing voltage that **lowers the voltage drop** across the resistor. Combining Ohm's Law with the KVL gives the voltage relation as $V_B = IR + \frac{Q}{C}$, where Q is the charge on the capacitor. Since the current is simply the transfer rate of the charge, this becomes a differential equation. Solving for charge and current yields the expressions $Q(t) = CV_B(1 - e^{-t/RC})$ and $I(t) = \left(\frac{V_B}{R}\right)e^{-t/RC}$. The factor RC in the exponent is referred to as the circuit's time constant. It is the amount of time required for the capacitor to charge up to 63.2% capacity.

If the battery is removed from the circuit after the capacitor is charged and the circuit is reconnected with just the resistor and capacitor, the capacitor will begin to drain at the same rate that it was charged. The current magnitude will follow the same equation as before, though it will be in the opposite direction. The new expression for the charge will be $Q(t) = CV_Be^{-t/RC}$.

Power in AC Circuits

Unlike DC circuits, the power provided by an AC voltage source is not constant over time. Generally, an AC source will provide voltage in a sinusoidal pattern, $V(t) = V_{max}\sin(\omega t)$. Similarly, the current will be given by $I(t) = I_{max}\sin(\omega t)$. From our known equations for power, this yields a power of $P(t) = RI_{max}{}^2\sin^2(\omega t)$. However, if we wish to find the average power or the amount of energy transmission after a given period of time, we need to find some way to average voltage and current. The root-mean-square (rms) method, as the name suggests, takes the square root of the time average of the squared value. For sinusoidal functions such as the voltage and current here, the rms value is the maximum value divided by the square root of 2. For voltage and current, $V_{rms} = \frac{V_{max}}{\sqrt{2}}$, and $I_{rms} = \frac{I_{max}}{\sqrt{2}}$. In this way, the average power can be found as $P_{avg} = V_{rms}I_{rms}$, which can also be stated $P_{avg} = \frac{V_{max}I_{max}}{2}$. A DC source with supplied voltage V_B will provide the same power over time as an AC source if $V_B = V_{rms}$.

Properties of Magnets

MAGNETS AND MAGNETISM

A **magnet** is any object or material, such as iron, steel, or magnetite (lodestone), that can affect another substance within its **field of force** that has like characteristics. Magnets can either attract or repel other substances. Magnets have two **poles**: north and south. Like poles repel and opposite poles (pairs of north and south) attract. The magnetic field is a set of invisible lines representing the paths of attraction and repulsion.

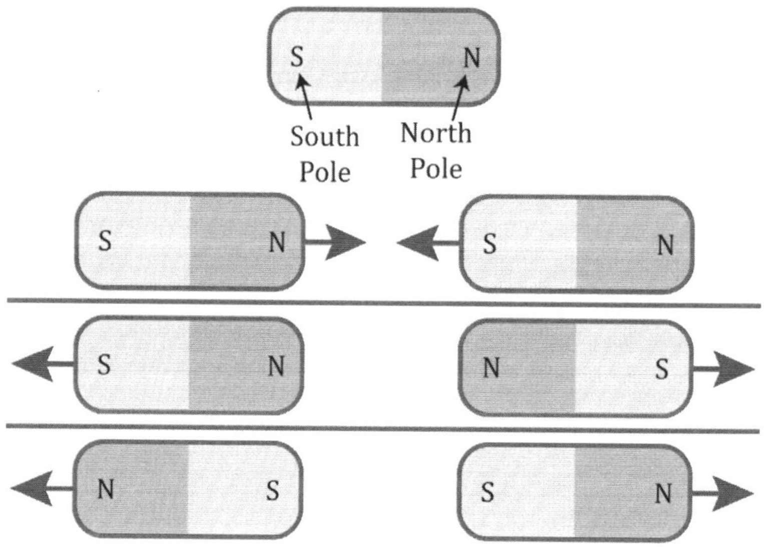

Magnetism can occur naturally, or ferromagnetic materials can be magnetized. Certain matter that is magnetized can retain its magnetic properties indefinitely and become a permanent magnet. Other matter can lose its magnetic properties. For example, an iron nail can be temporarily magnetized by stroking it repeatedly in the same direction using one pole of another magnet. Once magnetized, it can attract or repel other magnetically inclined materials, such as paper clips. Dropping the nail repeatedly will cause it to lose its magnetic properties.

Review Video: Magnets
Visit mometrix.com/academy and enter code: 570803

MAGNETIC FIELDS AND ATOMIC STRUCTURE

Motion of a charge produces a **magnetic field**. Within an atom, the negatively-charged electrons moving around the nucleus each generate a magnetic field. In most materials, these fields all perfectly oppose and cancel each other, but in certain elements (e.g., iron, cobalt, nickel) the fields are not completely canceled, which makes each atom a tiny magnet. The strength and direction of a magnetic field is known as the magnetic moment.

Pairs of electrons moving in opposite directions cancel each other out, creating a **net magnetic field** of zero. Materials that have an unpaired electron are magnetic. Those with a weak attractive force are referred to as **paramagnetic materials**, while **ferromagnetic materials** have a strong attractive force. A **diamagnetic material** has electrons that are paired, and therefore does not typically have a magnetic moment. There are, however, some diamagnetic materials that have a weak magnetic field.

A magnetic field can be formed not only by a magnetic material, but also by electric current flowing through a wire. When a coiled wire is attached to the two ends of a battery, for example, an **electromagnet** can be formed by inserting a ferromagnetic material such as an iron bar within the coil. When electric current flows through the wire, the bar becomes a magnet. If there is no current, the magnetism is lost. A **magnetic domain** occurs when the magnetic fields of atoms are grouped and aligned. These groups form what can be thought of as miniature magnets within a material. This is what happens when an object like an iron nail is temporarily magnetized. Prior to magnetization, the organization of atoms and their various polarities are somewhat random with respect to where the north and south poles are pointing. After magnetization, a significant percentage of the poles are lined up in one direction, which is what causes the magnetic force exerted by the material.

Types of Waves and their Characteristics

Transverse and Longitudinal Waves

Transverse waves have oscillations that are **perpendicular** to the direction of motion. A light wave is an example of a transverse wave. A group of light waves traveling in the same direction will be oscillating in several different planes. Light waves are said to be polarized when they are filtered such that only waves oscillating in a particular plane are allowed to pass, with the remainder being absorbed by the filter. If two such polarizing filters are employed successively and aligned to allow different planes of oscillation, they will block all light waves.

Longitudinal waves are waves that oscillate in the **same direction** as their primary motion. Their motion is restricted to a single axis, so they may not be polarized. A sound wave is an example of a longitudinal wave.

Velocity, Amplitude, Wavelength, and Frequency

- The **velocity of a wave**, v, is the rate at which it travels in a given medium. It is defined in the same way that velocity of physical objects is defined, a change in position divided by a change in time. A single wave may have a different velocity for every medium in which it travels. Some types of waves, such as light waves, do not require a medium.
- **Amplitude**, A, is one measure of a wave's strength. It is half the verticle distance between the highest and lowest points on the wave, the crest and trough, respectively. The vertical midpoint, halfway between the crest and trough, is sometimes called an equilibrium point, or a node.
- The **wavelength**, λ, is the horizontal distance between successive crests or troughs, or the distance between the first and third of three successive nodes.
- **Frequency**, f, is the number of crests or troughs that pass a particular point in a given period of time. It is the inverse of the period, the time required for the wave to cycle from one crest or trough to the next. Frequency is generally measured in hertz, or cycles per second.

Velocity, wavelength, and frequency are not independent quantities. They are related by the expression $v = \lambda f$. Note that amplitude, however, is independent from these quantities.

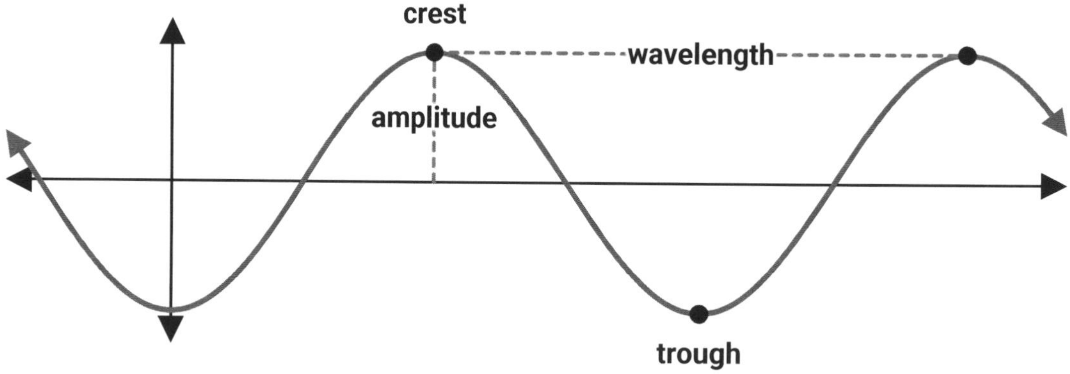

Intensity

The **intensity** I of a wave is equivalent to the flux through a given area over a period of time. It may also be defined as the energy density of a wave times its velocity. Intensity has units of watts per square meter. This can be seen in light waves as well. The intensity of light decreases as the distance from the light source increases. The inverse square law states that the intensity is inversely proportional to the square of the distance from the source. It is also directly proportional to the power P of the light source. This is shown mathematically by the expression $I = \frac{CP}{r^2}$, where C is the proportionality constant. This may be better understood by imagining the light waves emanating from a source as an expanding sphere. As their distance r from the source increases, the area over which they must divide themselves increases at a rate of $4\pi r^2$.

Standing Waves

A **standing wave** is the result of **interference** between two waves of the same frequency moving in opposite directions. These waves, although in constant motion, have certain points on the path where the amplitude is zero referred to as **nodes**. One example of a standing wave is a plucked guitar string. Since the string is attached at both ends, the fixed ends will be nodes. The primary tone will be that of the fundamental, or first harmonic, shown in the first figure below. It has a wavelength of twice the length of the string, L. The other three pictures below are those of the second through fourth harmonics. The nth harmonic has wavelength and frequency of $\lambda_n = \frac{2L}{n}$ and $f_n = \frac{nv}{2L}$, where v is wave velocity.

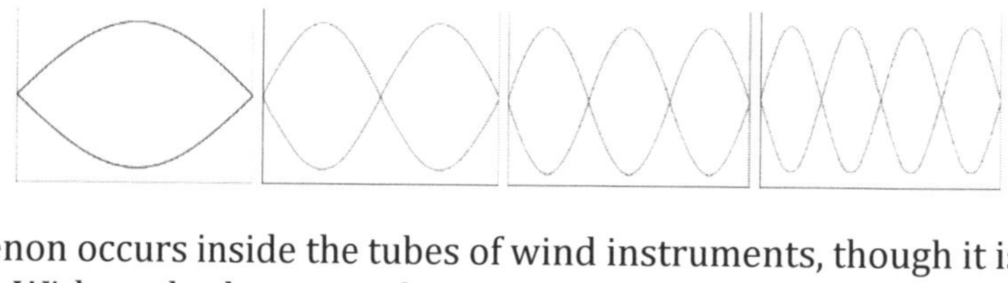

This same phenomenon occurs inside the tubes of wind instruments, though it is much more difficult to visualize. With a tube, however, there will be one or two open ends. Rather than a node, each open end will coincide with an **antinode**: that is, a crest or trough. For waves in a tube with two open ends, the wavelength and frequency calculations are the same as those for the plucked string. For the case with one open end, only the odd harmonics will be seen. The frequency of the nth harmonic becomes $f_n = \frac{nv}{4L}$, where n is odd.

Reflection, Refraction, Interference, and Diffraction of Waves

Reflection, Transmission, and Absorption

When light waves make contact with matter, they are either reflected, transmitted, or absorbed. If the light is **reflected** from the surface of the matter, the **angle** at which it hits the surface will be the same as the angle at which it leaves. If the ray of light is perpendicular to the surface, it will be reflected back in the direction from which it came.

When light is **transmitted** from one medium to another, its direction may be **altered** upon entering the new medium. This is known as **refraction**. The degree to which the light is refracted depends on the index of refraction, n, for each medium.

Light that is neither reflected nor transmitted will be **absorbed** by the surface and **stored as heat** energy. Because there are no ideal surfaces, most light and matter interaction will be a combination of two or even all three of these. Another result of imperfect surfaces is **scattering**, which occurs when waves are reflected in multiple directions. Rayleigh scattering is the specific case of a light wave being scattered by tiny particles that single out particular wavelengths. Dust particles in the atmosphere scatter primarily the blue wavelength of sunlight to give our sky a predominantly blue hue.

Review Video: Reflection, Transmission, and Absorption of Light
Visit mometrix.com/academy and enter code: 109410

Snell's Law

When light is transmitted from one medium to another, its direction may be altered upon entering the new medium. This is known as **refraction**. The degree to which the light is refracted depends on the index of refraction, n, for each medium. The **index of refraction** is a ratio of the speed of light in a vacuum to the speed of light in the medium in question, $n = \frac{c}{v_m}$. Since light can never travel faster than it does in a vacuum, the index of refraction is always greater than one. Snell's law gives the equation for determining the angle of refraction: $n_1 \sin(\theta_1) = n_2 \sin(\theta_2)$, where n is the index of refraction for each medium, and θ is the angle the light makes with the normal vector on each side of the interface between the two media.

We will examine a special case by trying to determine the angle of refraction for light traveling from a medium with $n_1 = 3$ to another medium with $n_2 = 1.5$. The light makes an angle $\theta_1 = 35°$ with the normal. Using Snell's law, we find that $\sin(\theta_2) = 1.15$. Since this is not mathematically possible, we conclude that the light cannot be refracted. This case is known as total internal reflection. When light travels from a more dense medium to a less dense medium, there is a minimum angle of incidence, beyond which all light will be reflected. This critical angle is $\theta_1 = \sin^{-1}\left(\frac{n_2}{n_1}\right)$. Fiber-optic cables make use of this phenomenon to ensure that the signal is fully reflected internally when it veers into the outer walls of the fiber.

Resonance and Natural Frequency

Every physical object has one or more **natural frequencies**, or frequencies at which it will naturally vibrate. The natural frequency is based on the object's dimensions, density, orientation, and other factors. If the object is acted on by a periodic force, it will vibrate at its natural frequency, regardless of the forcing frequency. If the excitation force is operating at the object's natural frequency, the object will experience **resonance**, in which the object receives all of the energy exerted by the excitation force. The amplitude of the vibration will increase rapidly and without bound until either the excitation force changes frequency or the natural frequency of the object is altered.

Diffraction and Dispersion

Diffraction occurs when a wave encounters a physical object. It includes phenomena such as bending, diverging, and other aperture effects. When light emerges from a single small slit, a rippling effect may be observed. The results of Young's double-slit experiment are due to diffraction as the light waves from these slits diverge. Similarly, light emerging from a circular aperture will project concentric light and dark rings due to diffraction. Diffraction grating is an arrangement of material whose reflective properties are intentionally varied at equally spaced intervals. Due to the arrangement, incident light is reflected in specific directions, known as diffraction orders, based on its wavelength.

Dispersion occurs when light consisting of multiple wavelengths enters a medium whose propagation behavior depends on the wavelength of transmitted light. This is what is observed when light passes through a prism, splitting it into its component colors.

Review Video: Diffraction of Light Waves
Visit mometrix.com/academy and enter code: 785494

Young's Double-Slit Experiment

Thomas Young's **double-slit experiment** visually demonstrated the interference between two sets of light waves. It consisted of shining light through two thin, closely spaced parallel slits and onto a screen. The interference between light waves from the two slits caused a pattern of alternately light and dark bands to appear on the screen, due to constructive and destructive interference, respectively. The dimensions of the experimental setup can be used to determine the wavelength of the light being projected onto the screen. This is given by the equation $\lambda = y\frac{d}{x}$, where y is the distance between the centers of two light bands, d is the distance between the slits, and x is the distance from the slits to the screen. Thin-film interference is caused when incident light is reflected both by a partially reflective thin layer on a surface and by the surface itself. This interference may be constructive or destructive.

Wave Superposition and Interference

The principle of **linear superposition** states that two or more waves occupying the same space create an effect equal to the sum of their individual amplitudes at that location. This is known as interference. If the resultant amplitude is larger than either individual amplitude, it is constructive interference. Similarly, if the interference reduces the effect, it is considered destructive.

Some special cases of interference are standing waves and beats, in which two waves having the same and nearly the same frequency, respectively, interfere with one another. Another concept related to interference is phase. If two waves with the same frequency are in phase, then they have perfectly constructive interference. The nodes in each wave will line up, as will the respective crests and troughs. If those same two waves are 180 degrees out of phase, they will experience perfectly destructive interference. The nodes will still line up, but each crest will be aligned with a trough, and vice versa. From this it can be seen that constructive interference results in a larger wave amplitude than destructive interference. If two identical waves are 180 degrees out of phase, the resultant wave will have zero amplitude. This effect is the design impetus for some noise-cancellation technology.

Doppler Effect

One common phenomenon of wave motion is the **Doppler effect**. It occurs when there is a **disparity** between the emitted frequency and the observed frequency of a wave. It is the caused by **relative motion** between the **wave source** and the **observer**. If the source and observer are both moving toward one another, the observed frequency is determined by the following equation: $f_o = f_e \frac{(v_w+v_o)}{(v_w-v_s)}$, where v_w is the speed of the wave. If the source or the observer is moving in the opposite direction, its sign must be reversed. The Doppler effect can occur with any wave (light, water, pressure, etc.), but it is most commonly observed when sound waves change pitch due to an observer's change in position relative to a loud train horn or emergency vehicle siren. The effect is also employed in the operation of speed-detecting radar guns. Microwaves are emitted at a known frequency and, after being reflected by the target, return at a different frequency, giving the object's speed.

Sound Waves

The **pitch of a sound** as it reaches one's ear is based on the frequency of the sound waves. A high-pitched sound has a higher frequency than a low-pitched sound. Like all waves, sound waves transmit energy. The rate at which this energy is transmitted is the sonic power. Loudness, or intensity of sound, is the sonic power received per unit area.

When a pair of sound waves with slightly different frequencies interfere with one another causing a periodic variation in sound intensity or a **beat**. The frequency of the variation, called the **beat frequency**, is equal to the difference between frequencies of the two sound waves. The phenomenon is used when tuning two instruments to one another. As the two pitches get closer, the beat frequency will become smaller and smaller until it disappears entirely, indicating that the instruments are in tune.

Review Video: Sound
Visit mometrix.com/academy and enter code: 562378

Electromagnetic Waves and Electromagnetic Spectrum

Electromagnetic Spectrum

The **electromagnetic spectrum** is the range of all wavelengths and frequencies of known electromagnetic waves. Visible light occupies only a small portion of the electromagnetic spectrum. Some of the common classifications of electromagnetic waves are listed in the table below with their approximate frequency ranges.

Classification	Freq. (Hz)
Gamma Rays	$\sim 10^{19}$
X-Rays	$\sim 10^{17} - 10^{18}$
Ultraviolet	$\sim 10^{15} - 10^{16}$
Visible Light	$\sim 10^{14}$
Infra-red	$\sim 10^{11} - 10^{14}$
Microwaves	$\sim 10^{10} - 10^{11}$
Radio/TV	$\sim 10^{6} - 10^{9}$

Electromagnetic waves travel at the speed of light, $c = 3 \times 10^8$ m/s. To find the wavelength of any electromagnetic wave, simply divide c by the frequency. Visible light occupies a range of wavelengths from approximately 380 nm (violet) to 740 nm (red). The full spectrum of color can be found between these two wavelengths.

Review Video: Electromagnetic Spectrum
Visit mometrix.com/academy and enter code: 771761

Review Video: Light
Visit mometrix.com/academy and enter code: 900556

Geometric Optics

Thin Lenses

A **lens** is an optical device that **redirects light** to either converge or diverge in specific geometric patterns. Whether the lens converges or diverges is dependent on the lens being **convex** or **concave**, respectively. The particular angle of redirection is dictated by the lens's focal length. For a **converging lens**, this is the distance from the lens that parallel rays entering from the opposite side would intersect. For a **diverging lens**, it is the distance from the lens that parallel rays entering the lens would intersect if they were reverse extrapolated. However, the focal length of a diverging lens is always considered to be negative. A thin lens is a lens whose focal length is much greater than its thickness. By making this assumption, we can derive many helpful relations.

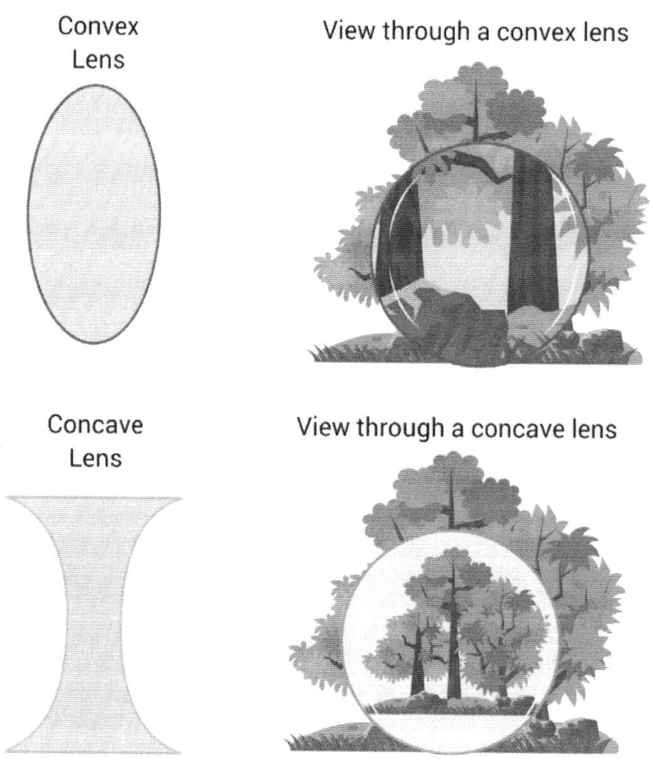

Real and Virtual Images

In optics, an **object's image** is what is seen when the object is viewed through a lens. The location of an object's image is related to the lens's **focal length** by the equation $\frac{1}{d_o} + \frac{1}{d_i} = \frac{1}{f}$, where f is the focal length, and d_o and d_i are the distance of the object and its image from the lens, respectively. A positive d_i indicates that the image is on the opposite side of the lens from the object. If the lens is a magnifying lens, the height of the object may be different from that of its image, and may even be inverted. The object's magnification, m, can be found as $m = \frac{-d_i}{d_o}$. The value for the magnification can then be used to relate the object's height to that of its image: $m = \frac{y_i}{y_o}$. Note that if the magnification is negative, then the image has been inverted.

Images may be either **real** or **virtual**. Real images are formed by light rays passing through the image location, while virtual images are only perceived by reverse extrapolating refracted light rays. Diverging lenses cannot create real images, only virtual ones. Real images are always on the opposite side of a converging lens from the object and are always inverted.

Concave Mirrors

Concave mirrors will create an image of an object in varying ways depending on the location of the object. The table below details the location, orientation, magnification, and nature of the image. The five object locations to be examined are between the mirror and the focal point (1), at the focal point (2), between the focal point and the center of curvature, or twice the focal point (3), at the center of curvature (4), and beyond the center of curvature (5).

Object	Image Location	Orientation	Magnification	Type
1	$d_i < 0$	upright	$m > 1$	virtual
2	none	none	none	none
3	$d_i > 2f$	inverted	$m < -1$	real
4	$d_i = 2f$	inverted	$m = -1$	real
5	$f < d_i < 2f$	inverted	$0 > m > -1$	real

Note in case 5 that the image may effectively be located at the focal point. This is the case for objects at extremely great, or near infinite, distances from the mirror. The magnification at these distances will be very small and a true infinite distance would result in a magnification of zero.

Plane Mirrors and Spherical Mirrors

Plane mirrors have very simple properties. They reflect only **virtual images**, they have no magnification, and the object's distance from the mirror is always equal to that of its image. Plane mirrors will also appear to reverse the directions left and right.

Spherical mirrors follow the same governing equations for finding image height, location, orientation, and magnification as do thin lenses; however, the sign convention for image location is reversed. A positive image location denotes that it is on the same side as the object. Spherical mirrors may be either **concave** or **convex**. Convex mirrors are by far the simpler of the two. They will always reflect virtual, upright images with magnification between zero and one. Concave mirrors have varying behavior based on the object location.

Simple Magnifier, the Microscope, and the Telescope

A simple magnifier, or commonly a **magnifying glass**, is a converging lens that creates an enlarged virtual image near the observer's eye. The object must be within a certain distance, about 25 cm or 10 inches, from the magnifier for it to operate properly. Otherwise, the image will be blurry.

A **microscope** is a magnifying device that is used to examine very small objects. It uses a series of lenses to capture light coming from the far side of the sample under examination. Often microscopes will have interchangeable magnification lenses mounted on a wheel, allowing the user to adjust the level of magnification by rotating in a different lens. Optical microscopes will generally be limited to a magnification of 1,500.

Telescopes are used to view very distant objects, most often celestial bodies. Telescopes use both lenses and mirrors to capture light from a distant source, focus it, and then magnify it. This creates a virtual image that is very much smaller than the object itself, and yet much larger than the object appears to the naked eye.

Prisms

Prisms are optical devices that alter the path or nature of light waves. Glass and plastic are the two most prevalent materials used to make prisms. There are three different types of prisms in common use. The most familiar of these is the dispersive prism, which splits a beam of light into its constituent wavelengths. For sunlight, this results in the full spectrum of color being displayed. These prisms are generally in the familiar triangular prism shape.

Polarizing prisms, as their name suggests, polarize light, but without significantly reducing the intensity, as a simple filter would. Waves that are oscillating in planes other than the desired plane are caused to rotate, so that they are oscillating in the desired plane. This type of prism is commonly used in cameras.

Reflective prisms are much less common than either of the others. They reflect light, often through the use of the total internal reflection phenomenon. Their primary use is in binoculars.

Heat Transfer

Heat transfer is the flow of thermal energy, which is measured by temperature. Heat will flow from warmer objects to cooler objects until an **equilibrium** is reached in which both objects are at the same temperature. Because the particles of warmer objects possess a higher kinetic energy than the particles of cooler objects, the particles of the warmer objects are vibrating more quickly and collide more often, transferring energy to the cooler objects in which the particles have less kinetic energy and are moving more slowly. Heat may be transferred by conduction, convection, or radiation. In **conduction**, heat is transferred by direct contact between two objects. In **convection**, heat is transferred by moving currents. In **radiation**, heat is transferred by electromagnetic waves.

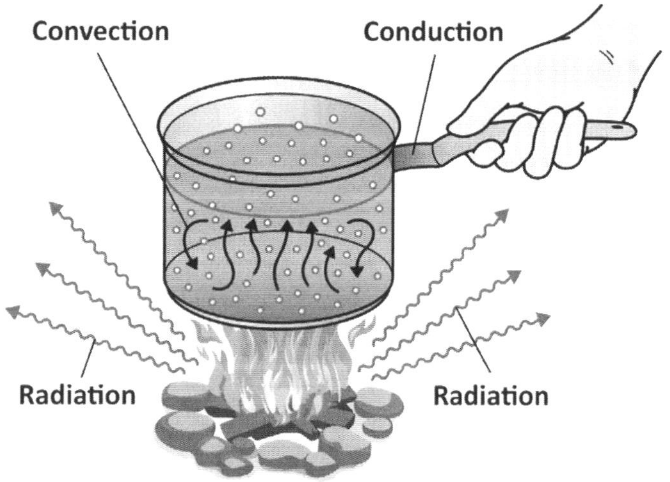

Review Video: Heat Transfer at the Molecular Level
Visit mometrix.com/academy and enter code: 451646

Convection

Heat always flows from a region of higher temperature to a region of lower temperature. If two regions are at the same temperature, there is a thermal equilibrium between them and there will be no net heat transfer between them. Convection is a mode of heat transfer in which a surface in contact with a fluid experiences a heat flow. The heat rate for convection is given as $q = hA\Delta T$, where h is the convection coefficient, and q is the heat transferred per unit of time. The convection coefficient is dependent on a number of factors, including the configuration of the surface and the nature and velocity of the fluid. For complicated configurations, it often has to be determined experimentally.

Convection may be classified as either free or forced. In free convection, when a surface transfers heat to the surrounding air, the heated air becomes less dense and rises, allowing cooler air to descend and come into contact with the surface. Free convection may also be called natural convection. Forced convection in this example would involve forcibly cycling the air: for instance, with a fan. While this does generally require an additional input of work, the convection coefficient is always greater for forced convection.

Conduction

Conduction is a form of heat transfer that requires contact. Since heat is a measure of kinetic energy, most commonly vibration, at the atomic level, it may be transferred from one location to another or one object to another by contact. The rate at which heat is transferred is proportional to the material's thermal conductivity k, cross-sectional area A, and temperature gradient $\frac{\Delta T}{\Delta x}$:

$$q = kA\left(\frac{\Delta T}{\Delta x}\right)$$

If two ends of a rod are each held at a constant temperature, the heat transfer through the rod will be given as $q = k\text{A}\left(\frac{T_H - T_L}{d}\right)$, where d is the length of the rod. The heat will flow from the hot end to the cold end. The thermal conductivity is generally given in units of $\frac{\text{W}}{\text{m K}}$. Metals are some of the best conductors, many having a thermal conductivity around 400 $\frac{\text{W}}{\text{m K}}$. The thermal conductivity of wood is very small, generally less than 0.5 $\frac{\text{W}}{\text{m K}}$. Diamond is extremely thermally conductive and may have a conductivity of over 2,000 $\frac{\text{W}}{\text{m K}}$. Although fluids also have thermal conductivity, they will tend to transfer heat primarily through convection.

Radiation

Radiation heat transfer occurs via electromagnetic radiation between two bodies. Unlike conduction and convection, radiation requires no medium in which to take place. Indeed, the heat we receive from the sun is entirely radiation since it must pass through a vacuum to reach us. Every body at a temperature above absolute zero emits heat radiation at a rate of $q = e\sigma AT^4$, where e is the surface emissivity and σ is the Stefan-Boltzmann constant. The net radiation heat-transfer rate for a body is given by $q = e\sigma A(T^4 - T_0^4)$, where T_0 is the temperature of the surroundings. Emissivity, which has a value between 0 and 1, is a measure of how well a surface absorbs and emits radiation. Dark-colored surfaces tend to have high emissivity, while shiny or reflective surfaces have low emissivity. In the radiation heat-rate equation, it is important to remember to use absolute temperature units, since the temperature value is being raised to a power.

Types of Energy

Chemical, Electrical, Electromagnetic, Nuclear, and Thermal Energy

Different types of energy may be associated with systems:

- **Chemical energy** is the energy that is stored in chemical bonds and intermolecular forces.
- **Electrical energy** is the energy associated with the movement of electrons or ions through a material.
- **Electromagnetic energy** is the energy of electromagnetic waves of several frequencies including radio waves, microwaves, infrared light, visible light, ultraviolet light, x-rays, and gamma rays.
- **Nuclear energy** is the binding energy that is stored within an atom's nucleus.
- **Thermal energy** is the total internal kinetic energy of a system due to the random motions of the particles.

Phase Transitions

States of Matter

The four states of matter are solid, liquid, gas, and plasma. **Solids** have a definite shape and a definite volume. Because solid particles are held in fairly rigid positions, solids are the least compressible of the four states of matter. **Liquids** have definite volumes but no definite shapes. Because their particles are free to slip and slide over each other, liquids take the shape of their containers, but they still remain fairly incompressible by natural means. **Gases** have no definite shape or volume. Because gas particles are free to move, they move away from each other to fill their containers. Gases are compressible. **Plasmas** are high-temperature, ionized gases that exist only under very high temperatures at which electrons are stripped away from their atoms.

Review Video: States of Matter
Visit mometrix.com/academy and enter code: 742449

Review Video: Properties of Liquids
Visit mometrix.com/academy and enter code: 802024

Review Video: States of Matter [Advanced]
Visit mometrix.com/academy and enter code: 298130

The following table shows similarities and differences between solids, liquids, and gases:

	Solid	Liquid	Gas
Shape	Fixed shape	No fixed shape (assumes shape of container)	No fixed shape (assumes shape of container)
Volume	Fixed	Fixed	Changes to assume volume of container
Fluidity	Does not flow easily	Flows easily	Flows easily
Compressibility	Hard to compress	Hard to compress	Compresses

Six Different Types of Phase Change

A substance that is undergoing a change from a solid to a liquid is said to be melting. If this change occurs in the opposite direction, from liquid to solid, this change is called freezing. A liquid which is being converted to a gas is undergoing vaporization. The reverse of this process is known as condensation. Direct transitions from gas to solid and solid to gas are much less common in everyday life, but they can occur given the proper conditions. Solid to gas conversion is known as sublimation, while the reverse is called deposition.

Review Video: Chemical and Physical Properties of Matter
Visit mometrix.com/academy and enter code: 717349

Phase Diagram and Critical Point

A **phase diagram** is a graph or chart of pressure versus temperature that represents the solid, liquid, and gaseous phases of a substance and the transitions between these phases. Typically, **pressure** is located on the vertical axis, and temperature is located along the horizontal axis. The curves drawn on the graph represent points at which different phases are in an equilibrium state. These curves indicate at which pressure and temperature the phase changes of sublimation, melting, and boiling occur. Specifically, the curve between the liquid and gas phases indicates the pressures and temperatures at which the liquid and gas phases are in equilibrium. The curve between the solid and liquid phases indicates the temperatures and pressures at which the solid and liquid phases are in equilibrium. The open spaces on the graph represent the distinct phases solid, liquid, and gas. The point at which the solid–liquid, solid–gas, and liquid–gas phase boundaries intersect is called the triple point. At the triple point, the solid, liquid, and gas phases all exist in equilibrium. The critical point, by contrast, is the endpoint of the liquid–gas coexistence curve, where the liquid and gas phases become indistinguishable and form a supercritical fluid.

LETTERED REGIONS OF A PHASE DIAGRAM

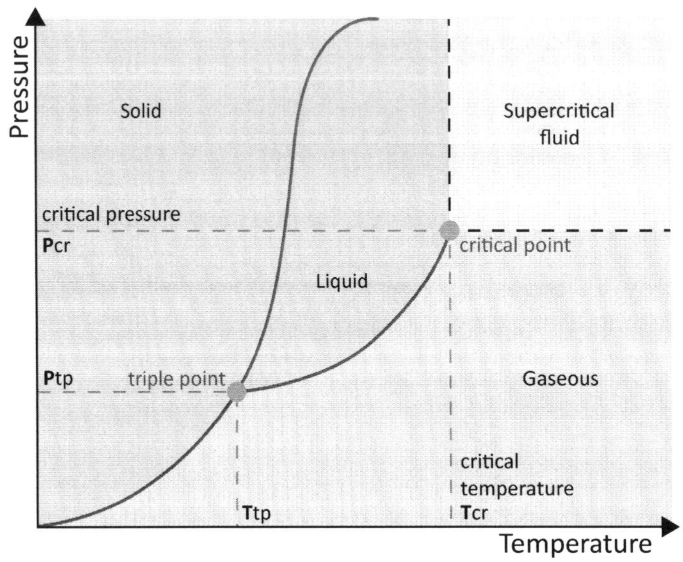

A—**Solid phase**: This is a region of high pressure and low temperature where the substance always exists as a solid.

B—**Liquid phase**: This is a region of pressure and temperature where the substance is in the liquid phase.

C—**Gas phase**: This is a region of pressure and temperature where the substance is in the gaseous phase.

D—**Sublimation point**: The portion of the curve that contains point D shows all the combinations of pressure and temperature at which the solid phase is in equilibrium with the gaseous phase.

E—**Triple point**: The point at which the solid, liquid, and gaseous phases are all in equilibrium.

F—**Boiling point**: The line that contains point F indicates all the combinations of pressure and temperature at which the liquid phase and gas phase are in equilibrium.

Laws of Thermodynamics

First Law

The **first law of thermodynamics** states that energy cannot be **created** or **destroyed**, but only **converted** from one form to another. It is generally applied as $Q = \Delta U + W$, where Q is the net heat energy added to a system, ΔU is the change in internal energy of the system, and W is the work done by the system. For any input of heat energy to a system, that energy must be either converted to internal energy through a temperature increase or expended in doing work. For a system that gives off heat, either the temperature of the system must decrease or work must be done on the system by its surroundings. By convention, work done by the system is positive while work done on the system is negative.

For instance, suppose a gas is compressed by a piston while the gas temperature remains constant. If we consider the gas to be the system, the work is negative, since the work is being performed on the gas. Since the temperature remains constant, $\Delta U = 0$. Thus, Q must be a negative quantity, indicating that heat is lost by the gas. Conversely, if the gas does positive work on the piston while remaining at a constant temperature, the gas must be receiving heat input from the surroundings.

Second Law

The **second law of thermodynamics** is primarily a statement of the natural tendency of all things toward disorder rather than order. It deals with a quantity called **entropy**, which is an inverse measure of the remaining useful energy in a system. If we take a system of a pot of hot water and an ice cube, the system entropy initially has a value of s_1. After the ice cube melts in the water and the system reaches an equilibrium temperature, the system has larger entropy value s_2, which is the maximum entropy for the system. The system cannot return to its initial state without work put into the system to refreeze the ice cube and reheat the water. If this is done and the system returns to a state with entropy s_1, then the entropy of the surroundings must at the same time increase by more than $s_2 - s_1$, since the net entropy from any process is always greater than zero. Reversible processes are those that may be accomplished in reverse without requiring additional work input. These processes do not exist in the real world, but can be useful for approximating some situations. All real processes are irreversible, meaning they require additional work input to accomplish in reverse. Another important concept is that of spontaneity, the ability of a process to occur without instigation. An ice cube located in an environment at a temperature above the freezing point will spontaneously melt. Although some processes can decrease system entropy at a cost to the entropy of the surroundings, all spontaneous processes involve an increase in the total entropy of the universe.

Third and Zeroth Laws

The **third law of thermodynamics** regards the behavior of systems as they **approach absolute zero temperature**. Actually reaching a state of absolute zero is impossible. According to this law, all activity disappears as molecules slow to a standstill near absolute zero, and the system achieves a perfect crystal structure while the system entropy approaches its minimum value. For most systems, this would in fact be a value of zero entropy. Note that this does not violate the second law since causing a system to approach absolute zero would require an immense increase in the entropy of the surroundings, resulting in a positive net entropy. This law is used to determine the value of a material's standard entropy, which is its entropy at the standard temperature of 25 °C.

The **zeroth law of thermodynamics** deals with thermal equilibrium between two systems. It states that if two systems are both in thermal equilibrium with a third system, then they are in thermal equilibrium with each other. This may seem intuitive, but it is an important basis for the other thermodynamic laws.

Review Video: Laws of Thermodynamics
Visit mometrix.com/academy and enter code: 253607

Entropy

Entropy (S) is the amount of **disorder** or **randomness of a system**. According to the second law of thermodynamics, systems tend toward a state of greater entropy. The second law of thermodynamics can also be stated as $\Delta S > 0$. Processes with positive changes in entropy tend to be spontaneous. For example, melting is a process with a positive ΔS. When a solid changes into a liquid state, the substance becomes more disordered; therefore, entropy increases. Entropy also will increase in a reaction in which the number of moles of gases increases due to the amount of disorder increasing. Entropy increases when a solute dissolves into a solvent due to the increase in the number of particles. Entropy increases when a system is heated due to the particles moving faster and the amount of disorder increasing.

Spontaneous / Reversible Processes

Some chemical processes are **spontaneous**. According to the second law of thermodynamics, systems or processes always **tend to a state of greater entropy** or lower potential energy. Some exothermic chemical systems are spontaneous because they can increase their stability by reaching a lower potential energy. If processes or reactions have products at a lower potential energy, these processes tend to be spontaneous. Spontaneous reactions have only one direction as given by the second law of thermodynamics. Spontaneous processes go in the direction of greater entropy and lower potential energy. To be reversible, a reaction or process has to be able to go back and forth between two states. A spontaneous process is irreversible.

Concept of Change in Enthalpy

All chemical processes involve either the release or the absorption of heat. Enthalpy is this heat energy. **Enthalpy** is a state function that is equivalent to the amount of heat a system exchanges with its surroundings. For **exothermic processes**, which release heat, the change in enthalpy (ΔH) is negative because the final enthalpy is less than the initial enthalpy. For **endothermic processes**, which absorb heat, the change in enthalpy (ΔH) is positive because the final enthalpy is greater than the initial enthalpy.

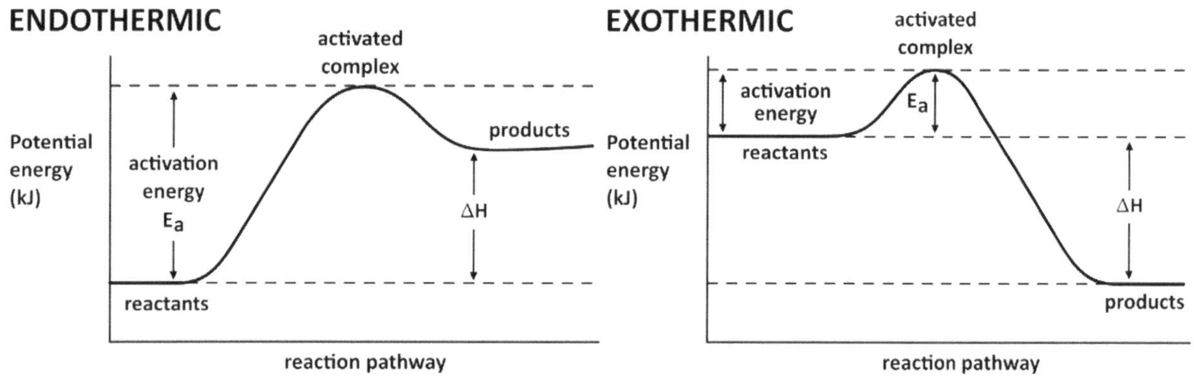

Review Video: Enthalpy
Visit mometrix.com/academy and enter code: 233315

Gibbs Energy

Gibbs energy (G), also known as Gibbs free energy, is the energy of the system that is available to do work. Gibbs energy determines the **spontaneity** of chemical and physical processes. Some processes are spontaneous because $\Delta H < 0$ or because $\Delta S > 0$. If one of the conditions is favorable but the other condition is not favorable, Gibbs energy can be used to determine if a process is spontaneous. Gibbs energy is given by $G = H - TS$. For processes that occur at constant temperature, $\Delta G = \Delta H - T\Delta S$. If ΔG is equal to zero, then the reaction is at equilibrium and neither the forward nor the reverse reaction is spontaneous. If ΔG is less than zero, then the forward reaction is spontaneous. If ΔG is greater than zero, then the reverse reaction is spontaneous.

Modern Physics and Additional Topics

Wave-Particle Duality and Heisenberg Uncertainty Principle

Wave-particle duality is the insight of quantum mechanics that states that energy will behave with the characteristics of both a **particle** and a **wave**. For most of the history of physics, it was believed that light was composed of electromagnetic waves and electrons were tiny particles of matter. However, experiments with light have created situations in which light will behave as if it were a particle (called a *photon*), and other experiments have suggested that photons will often behave as if they were waves. Essentially, quantum mechanics was created to resolve this conundrum. The result has been a series of theories, including the de Broglie hypothesis, that try to unify these seemingly contradictory attributes of matter.

One important measurement issue that arises from this dual nature is the **Heisenberg uncertainty principle**. This principle states that the position and linear momentum cannot be accurately measured beyond a certain level. Specifically, the minimum uncertainty in measuring the position, x, and linear momentum, p, in a given dimension is dictated by the relation $(\Delta x)(\Delta p) \geq \frac{h}{4\pi}$, where h is Planck's constant.

Photoelectric Effect

The **photoelectric effect** is the emission of electrons by substances when light falls on their surfaces. One of the main inspirations for the development of quantum theory was the inability of the standard theory of electromagnetic radiation to fully explain the photoelectric effect. Einstein declared that the incident light is composed of discrete particles of energy, known as **quanta**. The quanta of energy in light are known as **photons**. The energy of each photon is proportional to its frequency according to the equation $E = hf$, where E is energy, h is Planck's constant, and f is the frequency. When light is incident on a portion of an electric circuit, a current may be induced in the circuit. One property associated with this effect is stopping potential. This value is dependent on both the surface metal and the frequency of the incident light. Light of a given frequency will induce a current only if it does not have to overcome more potential in the circuit than the stopping potential. The stopping potential, V_0, is calculated by the equation $eV_0 = hf - \varphi$, where e is the elementary charge and φ is the work function of the metal. If $hf - \varphi$ is calculated in electron volts, V_0 is simply the equivalent number of volts.

De Broglie's Hypothesis

The de Broglie hypothesis is the assertion that all matter has a **wave-like nature**. According to the hypothesis, it is not just subatomic particles that exhibit wave properties; all objects do. This insight of de Broglie was confirmed by experiments that fired electrons at a very high speed at a crystalline nickel target. The diffraction of the electrons upon impacting the target was consistent with the diffraction exhibited by waves when passing through a slit with a width approximately the same as the wavelength of the wave. From these experiments, he produced two relations for an electron's frequency, f, and wavelength, λ, similar to those for photons: $f = \frac{E}{h}$ and $\lambda = \frac{h}{p}$, where E is the electron's energy, p is its linear momentum, and h is Planck's constant.

Michelson-Morley Experiment

The Michelson-Morley experiment proved that there is no substance like **ether** in outer space. It involved the use of a Michelson interferometer, a device that measures length to a great degree of precision by means of interference fringes. Basically, an interferometer sends two beams of light out, splits them at right angles to one another, and then brings them back to a central location with a mirror. Any very minor shift in the position of the beams will be seen as a shift in the interference fringes. Michelson and Morley wanted to use this device to determine the characteristics of the "luminiferous aether" wind that blew through outer space and affected the transmission of light, but instead they ended up disproving the existence of the ether altogether. They were also able to conclude from this experiment that the measured velocity of light is independent of the observer's reference-frame velocity.

Einstein's Theory of Relativity

Relativity is composed of special relativity and general relativity. **Special relativity** relates that those observers in inertial reference frames, in uniform motion relative to each other, cannot perform experiments to find out which is stationary. This is the principle of relativity, which says that regardless of an observer's velocity or position in the universe, all physical laws will appear constant. It was in this context that Einstein found that the speed of light in a vacuum had to be the same for all the observers despite their motion or the motion of the light source. **General relativity** is a geometrical theory that reasons that the presence of mass and energy will curve space-time, a model that combines mass and energy to form the space-time continuum, and that the curvature will affect the path of free particles. This includes the path of light. It uses differential geometry and the generalized quantity of tensors to describe gravitation without using the force of gravity. The theory postulates that all observers should be equivalent, not only those that move with uniform speed.

Lorentz Transformations and Equations

Because of the phenomena associated with Einstein's theory of relativity, measurements taken from **reference frames** traveling at high velocities may noticeably differ from those taken in a **stationary reference frame**. These differences in observation may be reconciled using Lorentz transformations. In the equations that follow, all quantities with a subscript zero represent those quantities as measured in a stationary frame. The primary conversion factor in these equations is the Lorentz factor (γ):

$$\gamma = \frac{1}{\sqrt{1 - \frac{v^2}{c^2}}}$$

The equations for length contraction and time dilation both use this factor. $L = \frac{L_0}{\gamma}$, where L is the observed length of an object in the direction of the frame's velocity. When observed from a high-velocity frame, objects will appear shorter. Also, $\Delta t = \Delta t_0 \gamma$, where Δt is elapsed time in a stationary frame as observed from a high-velocity frame. This means that from the high-velocity frame, time will seem to pass more quickly in the stationary frame.

One further equation relating high-velocity and stationary-frame measurements is velocity addition. For those velocities encountered in everyday life, an observer traveling at velocity, v, who measures an object's velocity as u', traveling in the same direction, will reasonably assume that the object's velocity in a stationary frame is $u = v + u'$. For velocities significant relative to the speed of light, c, the equation becomes $u = \frac{(v+u')}{(1+vu'/c^2)}$.

Simultaneous Events

Let us imagine a situation in which one **stationary observer** records two events that happen at the same time. If another observer moving at a **constant velocity** also records these two events, it is unlikely that the moving observer will record these two events as having happened simultaneously. In other words, two observers who are in relative motion will not generally agree as to whether two events are simultaneous. Neither observer is objectively right or wrong. We may therefore conclude that simultaneity is not an absolute concept but a relative one. It depends on the state of motion of the observer. Of course, since in most cases the speed of the observers will be a great deal less than the speed of light, this lack of simultaneity will be too small to notice.

Nuclear Binding Energy

The **nuclear binding energy** of an atom is the energy that would be required to **disassemble** the nucleus into its constituent nucleons. They are held together by a strong nuclear force in the nucleus. Nuclear binding energy may be calculated by determining the difference in mass between the nucleus and the sum of the masses of its constituent particles. This mass, m, is converted to energy by the equation $E = mc^2$, where c is the speed of light in a vacuum.

Nuclei may be transformed by a **rearrangement of nucleons**. These nuclear transformations may occur by many different means, including radioactive decay, nuclear fusion, and nuclear fission. In nuclear fusion, two light nuclei merge into a single nucleus that is heavier. In nuclear fission, a single large nucleus divides into two or more smaller nuclei. In either case, if the mass of the nuclei before transformation is greater than the mass after transformation, then it is an exothermic process. Conversely, if the mass is greater after transformation, the process is endothermic. Nickel and iron have the most stable nuclei of any elements, having the largest binding energies.

Blackbody Radiation

A **black body** is an ideal black substance that will absorb all radiation and reflect none of the radiation energy that falls on it. Powdered carbon is the closest real approximation of a black body. Because a black body is a perfect absorber of radiation, it is also a perfect emitter of radiation. The distribution of radiant energy in a black body according to wavelength will depend on the absolute temperature of the body: the higher the temperature, the lower the wavelength at which energy is distributed as a maximum. Blackbody radiation was used by Max Planck to develop the quantum theory of mechanics in 1901.

Elementary Particles

The two basic types of **elementary particles** are bosons, which have integer spin, and fermions, which have half-integer spin. There are a few different types of bosons, but the type most commonly encountered are photons, which make up the full spectrum of light.

There are only two types of fermions: leptons and quarks. Both leptons and quarks have antiparticles as well, with opposite charge.

- **Leptons** may be one of three different flavors: muon, tauon, or electron. Each of these is accompanied by a small electrically neutral particle called a neutrino, also differentiated by the same three flavors. Each lepton has a charge of -1, while its antiparticle has a charge of $+1$. The electron's antiparticle is the positron.
- **Quarks** are most commonly encountered as the constituent particles of nucleons. There are six different flavors of quark; the two most common are *up*, having a charge of $+\frac{2}{3}$, and *down*, having a charge of $-\frac{1}{3}$. Neutrons consist of one up quark and two down quarks, while protons have two up quarks and one down quark.

Chapter Quiz

Ready to see how well you retained what you just read? Scan the QR code to go directly to the chapter quiz interface for this study guide. If you're using a computer, simply visit the online resources page at **mometrix.com/resources719/ssregphysics** and click the Chapter Quizzes link.

Regents Practice Test #1

Want to take this practice test in an online interactive format?
Check out the online resources page, which includes interactive practice questions and much more: **mometrix.com/resources719/ssregphysics**

1. Starting from rest, a bicyclist accelerates in one direction at a constant 2 m/s^2. What is his instantaneous speed after 10 seconds?

a. 2 m/s
b. 5 m/s
c. 20 m/s
d. 40 m/s

2. Electrical wires are often made of copper covered with rubber. Which of the following best describes the reason for this?

a. Copper and rubber are both conductors
b. Copper and rubber are both insulators
c. Copper is a conductor; rubber is an insulator
d. Copper is an insulator; rubber is a conductor

3. A merry-go-round three meters in diameter takes 20 seconds to make a full rotation with no external forces acting on it. What is the linear speed of a horse at the edge of the merry-go-round?

a. 0.15 m/s
b. 0.47 m/s
c. 0.24 m/s
d. 0.94 m/s

4. If the average speed of the molecules in a gas increases, which of the following *must* be true?

a. The temperature of the gas increases
b. The pressure of the gas increases
c. The volume of the gas increases
d. The volume of the gas decreases

5. A catapult flings a stone with an initial velocity of 10 m/s at an angle of 40° from the horizontal. Assuming that the stone lands at the same altitude as its starting point and ignoring air resistance, how far away from the catapult will the stone land? Record your answer in meters and bubble in your answer to the nearest tenth on the answer document.

Question 6 pertains to the following graph of displacement from equilibrium versus time for a point on a vibrating string:

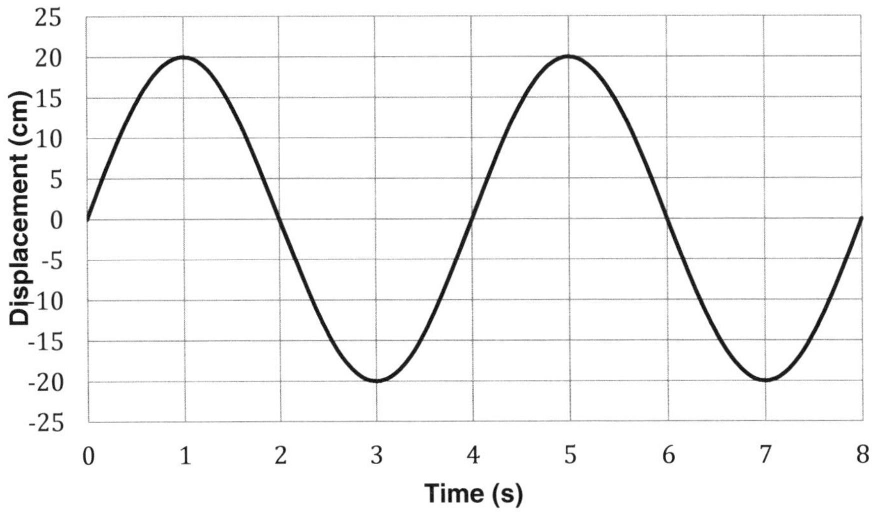

6. Which of the following characteristics of the wave *cannot* be determined from the graph?

a. Amplitude
b. Frequency
c. Period
d. Wavelength

7. A rock rests on a table. Which of the following is the reaction to the pull of the Earth's gravity on the rock?

a. The pull of the rock's gravity on the Earth
b. The pull of the Earth's gravity on the table
c. The normal force exerted on the rock by the table
d. The force of friction between the rock and the table

8. Which of the following scientists is *not* known for having played an important role in the study of electromagnetism?

a. Niels Bohr
b. Charles-Augustin de Coulomb
c. Michael Faraday
d. James Clerk Maxwell

9. A roller coaster car travels on a frictionless track along a flat section before entering a loop the top of which is ten meters higher than the flat section. What is the minimum speed at which the car must be traveling along the flat section in order to reach the top of the loop?

a. 5 m/s
b. 7 m/s
c. 10 m/s
d. 14 m/s

10. Which of the following best describes the image of a distant object as seen through a thin convex lens?

a. Real and upright
b. Real and inverted
c. Virtual and upright
d. Virtual and inverted

11. A metal block hangs from a spring. Which of the following is a correct force-body diagram for the forces acting on the block?

a.
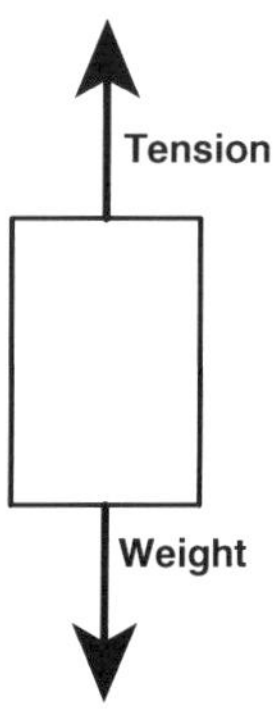

b.
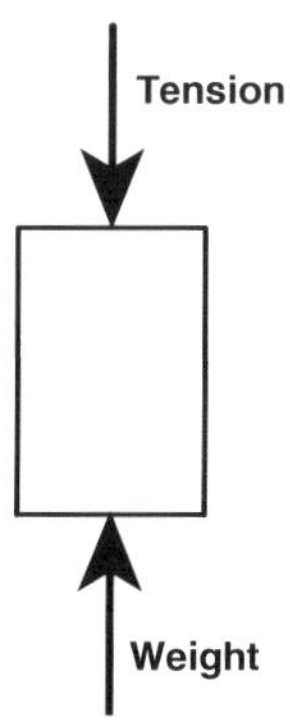

c.
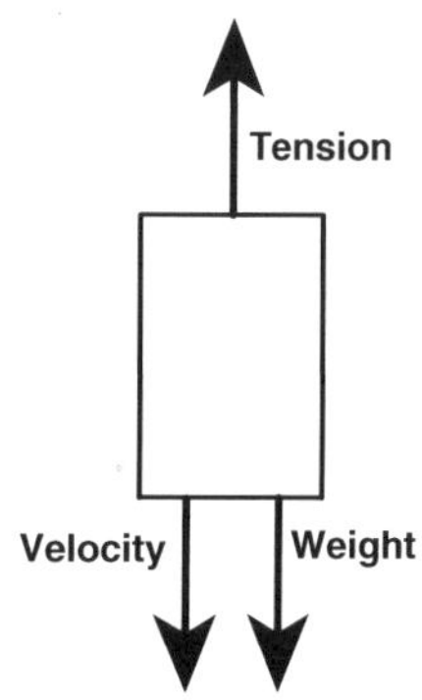

d.
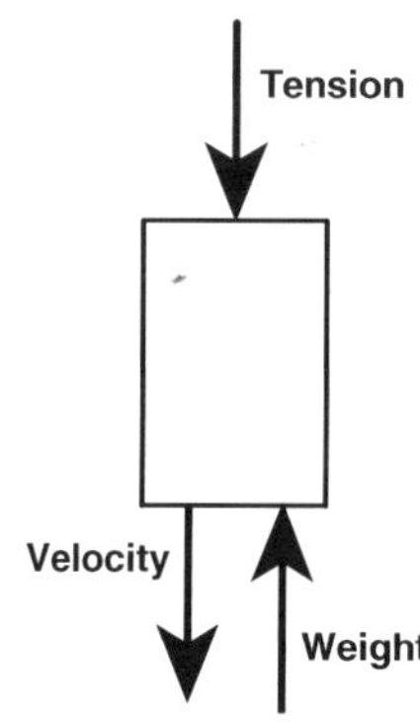

12. The mass of the planet Uranus is 8.7×10^{25} kg. The mass of the Sun is 2.0×10^{30} kg. The distance between Uranus and the Sun at one point in its orbit is about 2.9×10^{9} km. What is the magnitude of the gravitational force between the Sun and Uranus at this point?

a. 4.0×10^{36} N
b. 4.0×10^{33} N
c. 1.4×10^{27} N
d. 1.4×10^{21} N

13. A crane lifts a crate 10 meters off the ground and then lowers it onto a platform 6 meters above the ground. If the crate has a weight of 1000 N, what is the net work done by the crane?

a. 14000 J
b. 10000 J
c. 6000 J
d. 4000 J

14. The AC voltage across the wires on the left side of the transformer diagrammed here is 150 V at its peak. What is the peak voltage across the wires on the right side?

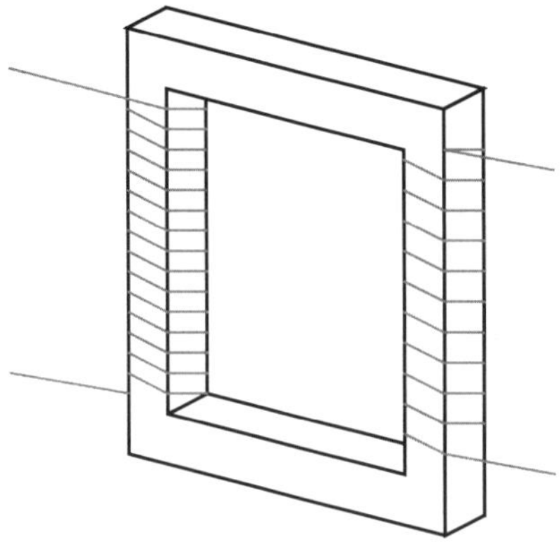

a. 15 V
b. 100 V
c. 150 V
d. 225 V

15. An elevator has a mass of 500 kg and can carry a maximum load of 1500 kg. What power is necessary to make the fully loaded elevator rise at a speed of 2.5 m/s? Record and bubble in your answer to the nearest kilowatt on the answer document.

16. Shown below are the approximate emission spectra of some common elements.

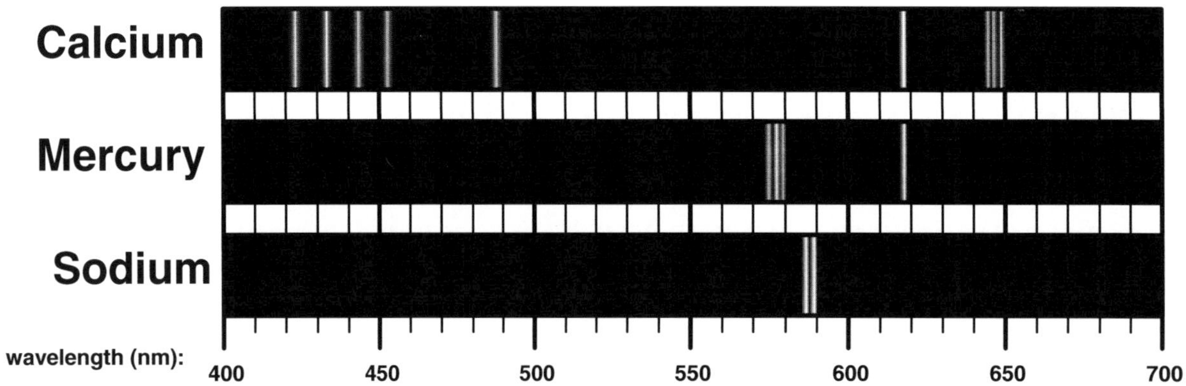

Using this information, state what elements you would expect a sample to contain that showed the following emission spectrum.

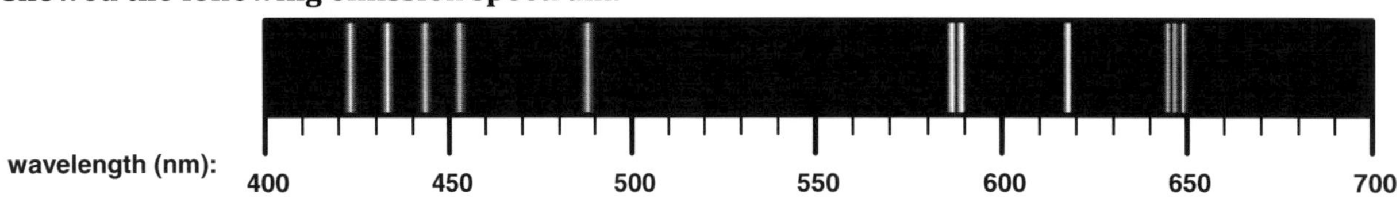

a. Calcium and mercury
b. Calcium and sodium
c. Mercury and sodium
d. Calcium, mercury, and sodium

17. Which of the following graphs most accurately displays velocity *v* versus time *t* of a ball rolling down a constant slope?

a.

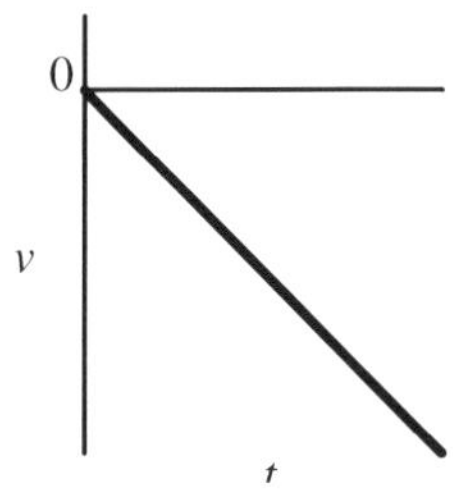

b.

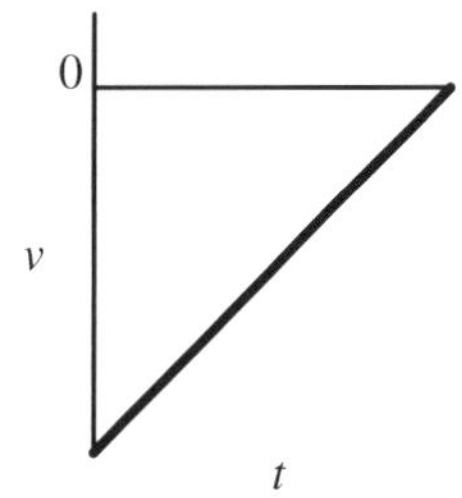

c.

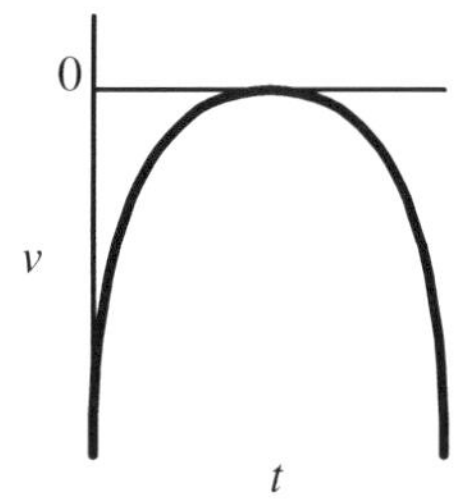

d.

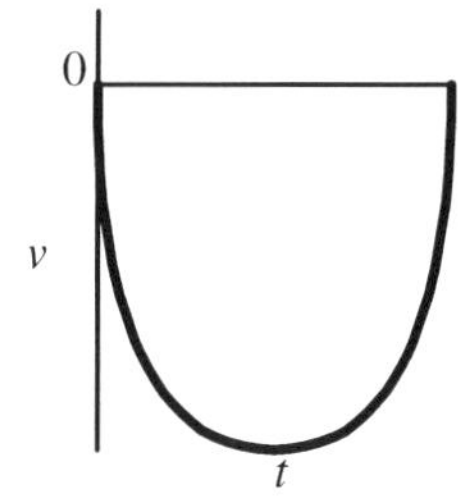

18. A soccer ball with a mass of 0.4 kg rolls toward a soccer player at a speed of 1 m/s. He kicks the ball, giving it a speed of 8 m/s in the opposite direction. What impulse did his kick produce on the soccer ball?

a. 0.4 kg m/s
b. 2.8 kg m/s
c. 3.2 kg m/s
d. 3.6 kg m/s

19. Which of the following best describes light and sound waves?

a. Light and sound are both transverse waves
b. Light and sound are both longitudinal waves
c. Light is a transverse wave; sound is a longitudinal wave
d. Light is a longitudinal wave; sound is a transverse wave

20. Three students pull ropes attached to a ring as shown in the diagram below. One student pulls due south with a force of 100 N, another pulls due east with an unknown force, and the third pulls in some direction north-northwest with a force of 115 N. The ring does not move. What is the magnitude of the unknown force?

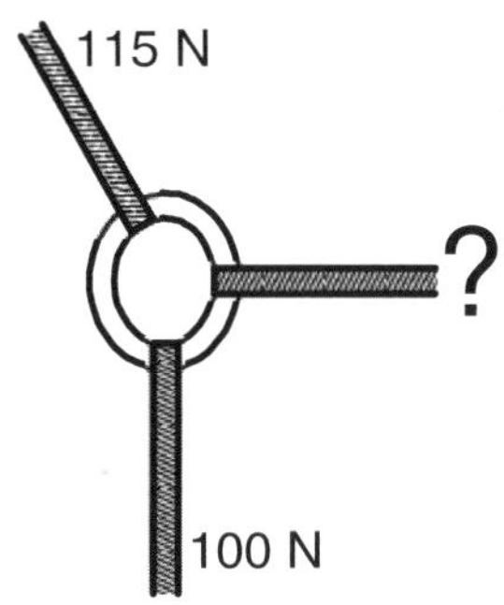

a. 15 N
b. 57 N
c. 81 N
d. 108 N

21. Which of the following items do *not* rely directly on magnetic forces to operate?

a. Cassette tapes
b. Compact discs
c. Compasses
d. Maglev trains

22. When you walk barefoot on a hot sidewalk, what process is primarily responsible for heat transfer from the sidewalk to your foot?

a. Conduction
b. Convection
c. Radiation
d. None of the above.

23. Which of the following observations provides the best evidence that sound can travel through solid objects?

a. Sound waves cannot travel through a vacuum.
b. The atoms of a solid are packed tightly together.
c. If you knock on a solid object, it makes a sound.
d. You can hear a sound on the other side of a solid wall.

24. A cannon is recessed in a pit so that the mouth of the cannon is at the same altitude as the ground. A cannonball is fired into the air and hits the ground 4 seconds later. What height did the cannonball reach at its peak?

a. 19.6 m
b. 39.2 m
c. 78.4 m
d. 156.8 m

25. The frequency of the light in a typical red He-Ne laser is 4.74×10^{14} Hz. What is its wavelength in nanometers? Record and bubble in your answer to the nearest nanometer on the answer document.

26. In the circuit pictured below, what is the current at point A?

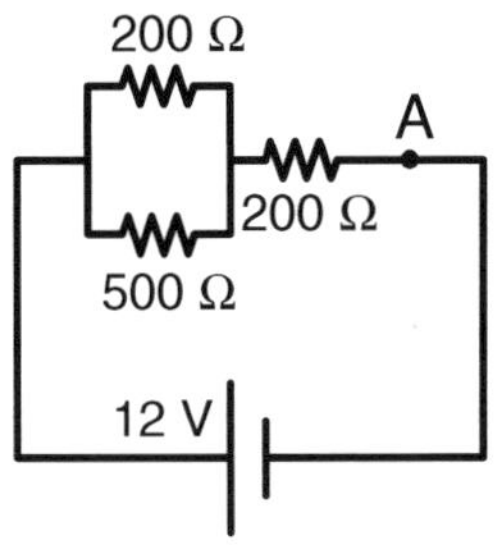

a. 13.3 mA
b. 35 mA
c. 60 mA
d. 154 mA

27. An inventor has an idea to create a plane that needs no fuel because it uses heat energy from the air, cooling the air to a lower temperature than anything in the plane and using the heat energy thus extracted to run the plane. Why wouldn't it actually be possible to build such a plane?

a. It violates conservation of energy
b. It violates conservation of mass
c. It violates conservation of momentum
d. It violates the law of entropy

28. Jim exerts a force of 320 N to push a heavy barrel along a floor surface with significant friction. He manages to impart to the barrel an acceleration of 0.13 m/s^2. If the barrel has a mass of 200 kg, what is the magnitude of the force of friction acting on the barrel?

a. 26 N
b. 147 N
c. 294 N
d. 320 N

29. Which of the following accurately describes an effect of the weak nuclear force?

a. It binds quarks into protons
b. It binds nucleons together into atomic nuclei
c. It binds protons to electrons to form atoms
d. It causes subatomic particles to decay

30. Two hydrogen nuclei fuse into a helium nucleus, releasing a burst of energy. If you could measure the masses before and after the nuclear reaction with an extremely sensitive scale, which of the following would you expect to find?

a. The two hydrogen nuclei have a slightly larger total mass than the helium nucleus
b. The two hydrogen nuclei have a slightly smaller total mass than the helium nucleus
c. The two hydrogen nuclei have exactly the same total mass as the helium nucleus
d. The hydrogen nuclei and the helium nucleus are all massless

31. The mass of an electron is 9.1×10^{-31} kg. The mass of a proton is 1.6×10^{-27} kg. The charge of an electron is -1.6×10^{-19} C. What is the magnitude of the electromagnetic force between a proton and an electron that are 0.1 mm apart?

a. 1.7×10^{-40} N
b. 1.3×10^{-39} N
c. 2.3×10^{-20} N
d. 0.14 N

32. A submarine is cruising north, at a speed of 10 m/s relative to a nearby island. It fires a torpedo directly to its right (that is, at a right angle to its direction of motion) at a speed of 25 m/s relative to the submarine. What is the initial speed of the torpedo relative to the island?

a. 15 m/s
b. 20 m/s
c. 27 m/s
d. 35 m/s

33. A light ray passes from air into a block of amber as shown in this diagram below. What is the index of refraction of amber?

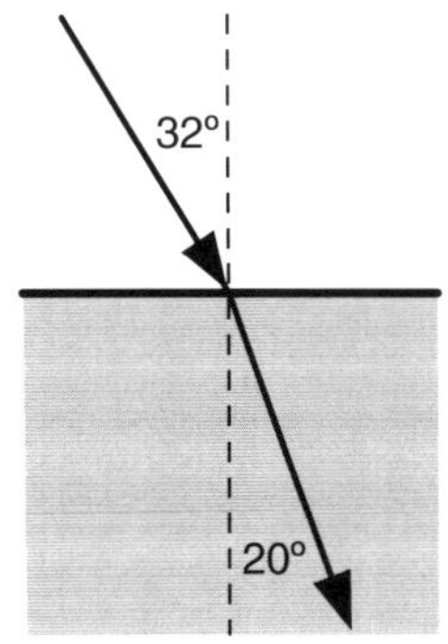

a. 1.11
b. 1.55
c. 1.60
d. 1.66

34. A bus is moving down a street at 10 m/s. A man walks to the back of the bus at a speed of 1 m/s, dragging a suitcase. What is the speed of the suitcase?

a. 0 m/s
b. 1 m/s
c. 9 m/s
d. It depends on the frame of reference

35. A rocket with a mass of 1000 kg is launched horizontally and propelled to a final velocity of 200 m/s. An identical rocket has a payload attached with a mass of an additional 500 kg. If both rockets have the same fuel efficiency, what will the final velocity of the second rocket be when it is launched horizontally? Record and bubble in your answer in m/s on the answer document, to the nearest tenth.

36. Which of the following best explains why medical imaging machines use x-rays instead of visible light?

a. X-rays have shorter wavelengths than visible light, which lets them penetrate matter more easily
b. X-rays have longer wavelengths than visible light, which lets them penetrate matter more easily
c. X-rays have shorter wavelengths than visible light, which means they are more energetic
d. X-rays have longer wavelengths than visible light, which means they are less energetic

37. The speed of a small wheeled robot is measured by dividing the distance between two marked points by the time the robot takes to travel between the two points. The distance is recorded as 1.000 meters, as measured by a meter stick that can measure to the nearest millimeter, and the time is recorded as 5.00 seconds, as measured with a stopwatch that can measure to the nearest 0.01 seconds. Which of the following best expresses the measurement of the robot's speed and its uncertainty?

a. 0.20000 m/s ± 0.000224 m/s
b. 0.20000 m/s ± 0.00045 m/s
c. 0.200 m/s ± 0.00045 m/s
d. 0.200 m/s ± 0.000224 m/s

38. Which two of the four fundamental forces were recognized as two manifestations of a single interaction and combined in a unified theory?

a. The strong and weak nuclear forces
b. Gravity and the strong nuclear force
c. Electromagnetism and the weak nuclear force
d. Gravity and electromagnetism

39. Which of the following correctly describes the relationship between the work done on an object and its change in kinetic energy?

a. The work done on an object is always greater than its change in kinetic energy
b. The work done on an object is always less than its change in kinetic energy
c. The work done on an object is always equal to its change in kinetic energy
d. The work done on an object may be greater than, less than, or equal to its change in kinetic energy

40. Which of the following best describes how quantum phenomena relate to the working of electron microscopes?

a. Light behaves as a particle, allowing the microscope to hit the observed object with one photon at a time
b. Electrons behave as waves, allowing beams of electrons to be diffracted by and reflect from and thereby "illuminate" objects
c. The uncertainty principle allows the microscope to determine an object's exact contours
d. Quantum entanglement ensures that the observed object is "entangled" with the observer

41. A scientist mixes two chemicals together, and they produce a violent reaction, generating considerable heat. Where did the thermal energy come from to heat up the chemicals?

a. The kinetic energy of the molecules in the chemicals
b. Potential energy inherent in the atomic bonds in the molecules of the chemicals
c. It was absorbed from the surrounding air
d. Nowhere; the energy was completely created by the reaction

42. Four synchronized photogates are set up on an inclined track as shown in the diagram below.

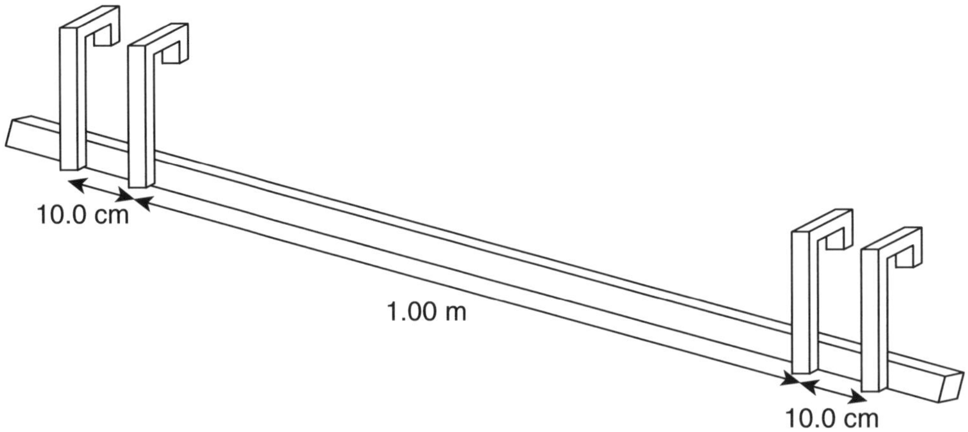

A metal cart slides along the track (with a constant acceleration), and each photogate records the time at which the cart passes through it as follows:

0 s	0.079 s	0.551 s	0.586 s

Which of the following best describes the acceleration of the cart?

a. 3.0 m/s^2
b. 7.0 m/s^2
c. 20 m/s^2
d. 35 m/s^2

43. Though oxygen most normally is found in diatomic form (O_2), it sometimes also occurs as monatomic oxygen (O) or as ozone (O_3). Which form would you expect to have the lowest specific heat (C_v)?

a. Monatomic oxygen
b. Diatomic oxygen
c. Ozone
d. All three forms should have the same specific heat.

44. Which of the following arrangements of four identical batteries should generate the highest voltage?

a. 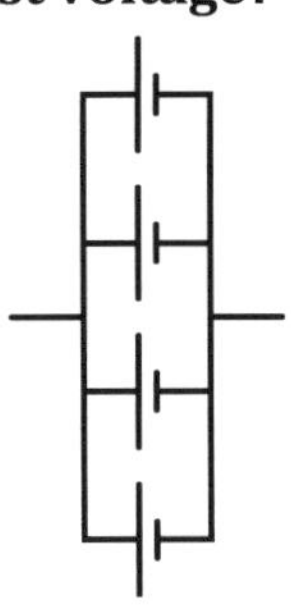

b. 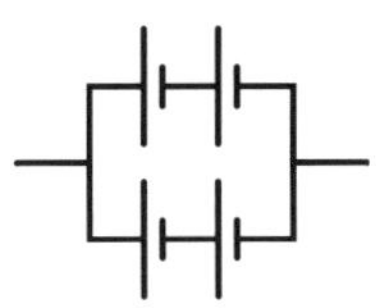

c. 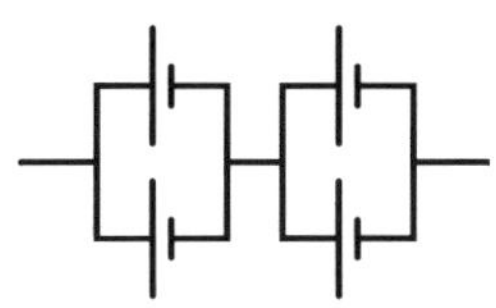

d. 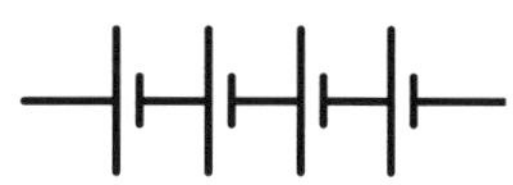

45. A train whistle has a frequency of 450 Hz (as heard by someone onboard the train). If the train is moving at 60 m/s, and the speed of sound is 340 m/s, what is the frequency in Hz, of the whistle as heard by someone standing in front of the train on a windless day? Record and bubble in your answer to the nearest tenth on the answer document.

46. The diagram below shows a simple DC electric motor, with the exception of the wires connecting it to the power source. To which part of the motor should those wires be attached?

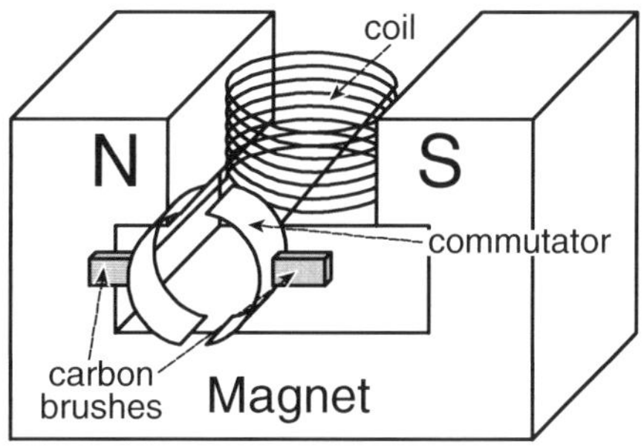

a. To the north and south poles of the magnet
b. To the two sides of the commutator
c. To the ends of the coil
d. To the carbon brushes

47. The photoelectric threshold frequency of gold is about 1.11×10^{15} Hz. A gold plate is configured so that a very sensitive ammeter measures the photoelectric current produced when light is shined on the plate. When an intense beam of light with a wavelength of 200 nm is directed at the gold plate, the ammeter measures a current of 2×10^{-6} A: What current would you expect to measure if a beam of light with half the intensity and twice the wavelength of the first beam is directed at the plate?

a. 4×10^{-6} A
b. 2×10^{-6} A
c. 1×10^{-6} A
d. 0 A

48. When a car brakes rapidly, passengers are thrown forward. Which physical law best describes why this occurs?

a. The law of conservation of energy
b. The law of entropy
c. The law of inertia
d. The law of relativity

49. A sled with a mass of 100 kg slides on an icy lake. It collides with another sled with a mass of 80 kg. Before the collision, the first sled was traveling at a speed of 4.0 m/s, and the second sled was stationary. After the collision, the first sled was traveling at a speed of 1.0 m/s. How fast was the second sled traveling after the collision?

a. 3.0 m/s
b. 3.8 m/s
c. 4.3 m/s
d. 5.0 m/s

50. Which of the following shows the correct way to connect an ammeter and a voltmeter to a circuit in order to measure the current through and voltage across a resistor?

a.

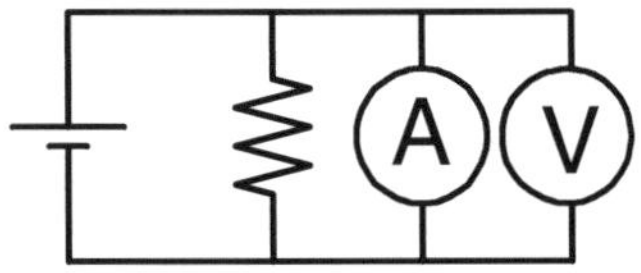

b.

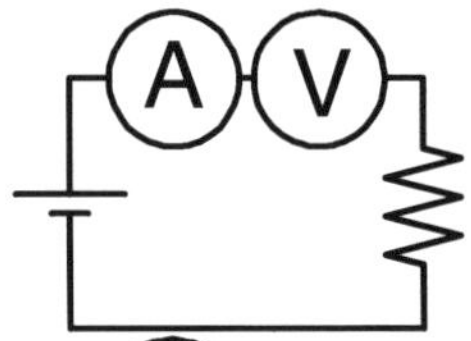

c.

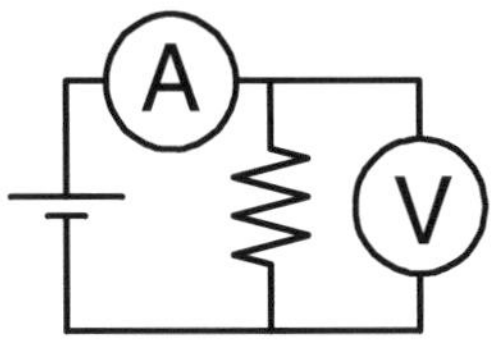

d.

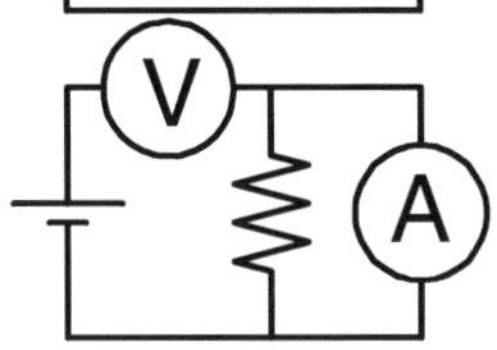

Answer Key and Explanations for Test #1

1. C: The formula for velocity given constant acceleration is $v = v_0 + at$. Since the bicyclist starts from rest, $v_0 = 0$. So $v = (2\ m/s^2)\ (10\ s) = 20\ m/s$.

2. C: A wire needs to be made of a conductive material to allow electricity to flow through it easily. Wires are coated, however, in an insulating material so that the circuit will not be shorted if the wire comes into contact with itself or with another conductor.

3. B: During one full rotation, the horse travels a distance $2\pi r = 2(3.14)\ (1.5\ m) = 9.42\ m$. The speed is then equal to distance divided by time, 9.42 m/20 s = 0.47 m/s.

4. A: The temperature of a gas is related to the average kinetic energy of the component particles. If the molecule speed increases, the kinetic energy increases, and the temperature must also increase by definition. Any of the other choices *could* be true, depending on factors such as whether the gas is in a sealed and rigid container, but only choice A *must* be true.

5. 10.0: Consider the horizontal and vertical components of the motion separately. The initial velocity in the horizontal direction is (10 m/s) (cos 40°) = 7.66 m/s; the initial velocity in the vertical direction is (10 m/s) (sin 40°) = 6.43 m/s. We can use the vertical component to calculate the time the stone is in flight using the equation $x = x_0 + v_0t + ½at^2$, where x and x_0 are both 0 m (since the stone starts and ends at the same altitude), v_0 is 6.43 m/s, and a is the acceleration due to gravity, -9.81 m/s². This yields (6.43 m/s) t = ½(9.81 m/s²) $t2$; solving for t yields either $t = 0$ (corresponding to its initial position) or $t = 1.31$ s. Since there is no acceleration in the horizontal direction, the total horizontal distance the stone travels in this time is simply (7.66 m/s) (1.31 s) = 10.0 m.

6. D: The amplitude is in this case simply the maximum displacement from equilibrium (20 centimeters). The period is the time in which the point completes one full cycle (4 seconds), and the frequency is just the inverse of the period (0.25 Hz). To find the wavelength, however, information about a different point that corresponds to this one, or about the speed of the wave, is required and not given, and D is the correct choice.

7. A: In an action-reaction force pair, the reaction force must be exerted *by* the object *on* which the action force is exerted, and *on* the object *by* which the action force is exerted. Since the action force is exerted *by* the Earth *on* the rock, the reaction force must be exerted *by* the rock *on* the Earth. The only choice that fits this criterion is A: (Note that it would have been just as valid to consider the pull of the rock's gravity on the Earth to be the action force, and the pull of the Earth's gravity on the rock to be the reaction force. The important thing is there are two equal and opposite forces; which is the action and which is the reaction is essentially arbitrary.)

8. A: Coulomb developed the formula for electromagnetic force now known as Coulomb's Law. Faraday developed the idea of the electromagnetic field. Maxwell worked out the unification of electricity and magnetism as aspects of a single phenomenon. Bohr, however, is a more recent scientist best known for his work on the structure of atoms which helped lay the foundation for quantum mechanics, not for having played a major role in the study of electromagnetism, and the answer is A.

9. D: There are several different ways to approach this problem, but perhaps the simplest is by conservation of energy. On the flat stretch, we can take the car's gravitational potential energy as zero, so its mechanical energy is purely kinetic: $KE = ½mv^2$. If the car just barely makes it to the top of the loop (like a projectile at the top of its arc), its velocity and therefore its kinetic energy are zero at that point, and its mechanical energy is purely gravitational potential energy: $PE = mgh$. Since energy is conserved, the energy at these two points must be equal: $½mv^2 = mgh$. The masses cancel, leaving $½v^2 = gh$, and solving for v yields $v = \sqrt{2gh} = \sqrt{2(9.8\text{m/s}^2)(10\text{m})} = \sqrt{196\text{m}^2/s^2} =$ 14 m/s.

10. B: The image of a distant object seen through a thin convex lens is real, because the light rays actually do converge at the location of the image, and inverted. The only choice with these characteristics is B: One way to see this is by tracing light rays, as in the following diagram (in which the black circles represent the focal length of the lens):

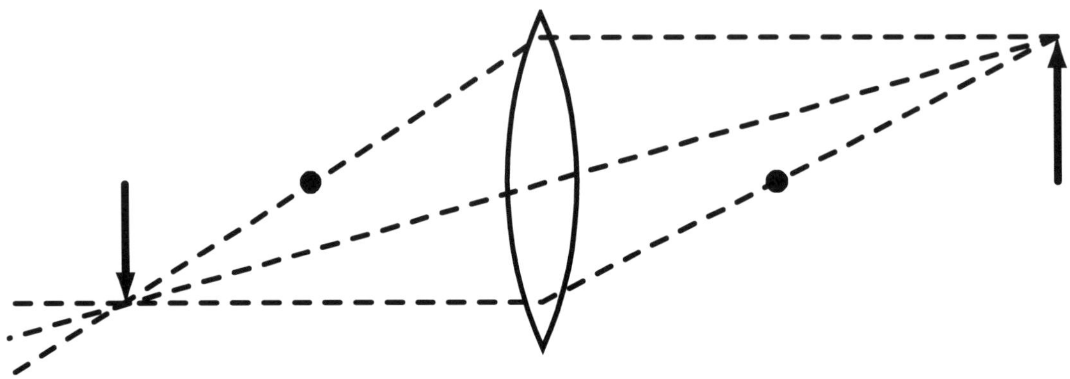

11. A: As described, there are two forces acting on the block: the tension in the spring pulling it upward, and the block's own weight (the force of gravity) pulling it downward. Only choice A depicts these forces correctly. Choice B has them acting in the wrong directions, choice C incorrectly adds velocity which is not a force and does not belong on a force diagram, and choice D combines the mistakes of B and C.

12. D: The equation for the gravitational force is $F = \frac{Gm_1m_2}{r^2}$. In order for the units to work out correctly and yield an answer in Newtons, r has to be in meters. We can easily convert, $2.9 \times 10^9\ km = 2.9 \times 10^{12}\ m$. We then have $F = \frac{\left(6.67\times10^{-11}\frac{\text{m}^3}{\text{kg}\cdot\text{s}^2}\right)(8.7\times10^{25}\text{kg})(2.0\times10^{30}\text{kg})}{(2.9\times10^{12}\text{m})^2} =$ $1.38 \times 10^{21}\ N$.

13. C: Net work done is determined by the change in energy. Since the crate is not moving in the initial or final state, the relevant energy is gravitational potential energy. From the ground, the final change in altitude of the crate is 6 meters, which corresponds to a potential energy change of $mg\Delta h$ = (1000 N)(6 m) = 6000 J, and the net work done by the crane is 6000 J, choice C: That the crane first raised the crate to an altitude of 10 m before lowering it to 6 m is irrelevant for finding the *net* work.

14. B: A transformer works by induced voltage; the varying voltage through the coil on one side induces a voltage in the coil in the other. The ratio of the voltages on the sides of an ideal transformer is equal to the ratio of the numbers of turns in the coils. In this case, there are 15 coils on the left-hand side, and 10 coils on the right-hand side, for a ratio of 15/10, or 1.5. This same ratio must hold between the voltages, so that $\frac{150\ V}{V_R} = 1.5$, giving a voltage on the right of V_R = 100 V.

15. 49 kWh: The total mass of the fully loaded elevator is equal to 500 kg + 1500 kg = 2000 kg. If the elevator is moving at 2.5 m/s, it moves 2.5 m in one second. The work done in that second is equal to the change in potential energy, which is $mg\Delta h$ = (2000 kg)(9.81 m/s^2)(2.5 m) = 49050 J. The power is equal to the work divided by the time, which is 49050 J/1 s = 49050 W, or 49 kW.

16. B: All the lines of the calcium spectrum are present in the unknown spectrum, including the notable low-wavelength lines not present in the mercury or sodium spectra. The double line at around 590 nm characteristic of the sodium spectrum is also present, so the sample must contain sodium. However, the lines from the mercury spectrum are *not* present in the unknown sample, most notably the easily recognizable triple line at about 580 nm. Therefore the unknown sample contains calcium and sodium, but does *not* contain mercury; this corresponds to choice B.

17. A: We would expect the velocity to increase over time at a constant rate. Although choice A shows what appears to be a decrease in velocity, it is actually increasing in the negative direction; as we expect, and the magnitude of the velocity is increasing, as the ball picks up speed rolling down the slope. Choice B shows the velocity starting with some non-zero magnitude which then decreases to zero, the opposite of our expectation, and is incorrect. Choice C shows the velocity slowing to zero and then increasing again, and choice D shows the velocity increasing from and then decreasing to zero. Neither of these two choices makes physical sense; they are also incorrect. Choice A is correct.

18. D: The impulse is equal to the change in momentum. The initial momentum is (0.4 kg)(1 m/s) = 0.4 kg·m/s towards the player. The final momentum is (0.4 kg)(8 m/s) = 3.2 kg·m/s in the opposite direction. The change is then 3.2 kg·m/s – (-0.4 kg·m/s), where the negative sign reflects the opposite directions), which equals 3.6 kg·m/s.

19. C: Light is an electromagnetic wave, and thus a transverse wave; its oscillation is perpendicular to its propagation. Sound is a longitudinal wave, alternating compressions and expansions of the medium it's traveling through. Choice C correctly represents this.

20. C: Since the ring isn't moving, the net force is zero. If we separate the force into perpendicular components, both components must be zero. If we consider the *x* direction to be to the right on the page, and the *y* direction to be upward, then one student is pulling completely in the +*x* direction, and another is pulling completely in the -*y* direction. Consider the *y* components first. One student is pulling with a force of 100 N in the -*y* direction, while another is pulling at an angle with a force of 115 N. The *y* components of these forces must cancel, and the *y* component of the 115 N force must be 100 N. This means the Pythagorean theorem can find the *x* component of the force at an angle: $\sqrt{(115\text{ N})^2 - (100\text{ N})^2}$ = 57 N in the -*x* direction. Since the *x* components of all the forces must also cancel, the unknown force must be 57 N in the +*x* direction, choice C.

21. B: Data is stored on cassette tapes by magnetizing the tapes. Compasses point north because of magnetic attraction to the Earth's magnetic pole. Maglev trains "float" because of magnetic repulsion between the trail and the rail. Choice B, compact discs, however, does not rely directly on magnetism, and is the correct choice; the data is stored in the form of small pits in the surface which affect the reflection of laser light.

22. A: Heat between objects in contact with each other is transferred by conduction, choice A. Convection is transfer by currents within a body of fluid, and radiation is the transfer of heat between objects *not* in contact, through light rays emitted by the hotter object and absorbed by the cooler one.

23. D: Sound cannot travel through a vacuum, though it doesn't necessarily follow that it *can* travel through solids. Nor does the fact sound can travel through a solid follow from the fact that the atoms are packed tightly together. The fact that a sound is produced by knocking on a solid object also does not prove sound can pass through the object. However, if you hear a sound on the other side of a solid wall, the sound must have traveled through the wall. Choice D is the best answer.

24. A: The cannonball's horizontal distance is not specified, but the horizontal and vertical components can be independently considered; this problem can be approached by considering only the vertical motion, and the easiest approach depends on recognizing the cannonball will reach its peak altitude exactly halfway through its arc. Thus, if the full trajectory takes four seconds, the cannonball takes two seconds to reach its peak, and two seconds to fall back to the ground. Knowing this, a formula for uniformly accelerated motion will calculate how high the cannonball could fall from in two seconds: $x - x_0 = v_0t + ½at^2 = ½(9.8\ m/s^2)(2\ s)^2 = 19.6\ m$, (recognizing that v_0 is zero at the top of the arc).

25. 633 nm: The speed of a wave is equal to wavelength times frequency, $v = f\lambda$. The speed of a light wave is $c = 3.00 \times 10^8$ m/s. The wavelength is therefore equal to $c / f =$

$(3.00 \times 10^8\ m/s) / (4.74 \times 10^{14}\ Hz) = 6.33 \times 10^{-7}$ m, or 633 nm.

26. B: The effective resistance of two or more resistors in parallel is equal to the reciprocal of the sum of their reciprocal resistances. The two resistors in parallel therefore have an effective resistance of $((200\Omega)^{-1} + (500\ \Omega)^{-1})^{-1} = 142.9\ \Omega$. Resistances in series simply sum, so the total resistance of the parallel element plus the second 200 Ω resistor is 142.9 Ω + 200 Ω = 342.9 Ω. Ohm's Law, $V = IR$, can be used to solve for $I = (12\ V)/(342.9\ \Omega) = 0.035\ A = 35\ mA$.

27. D: Conservation laws of mass and momentum do not apply here. The law of entropy is also known as the second law of thermodynamics, and can be stated in several different forms. One form, first developed by Lord Kelvin, states that it is impossible to convert heat into useful energy without producing more heat energy at another point in the system to heat up a low-temperature sink. If the air is cooled to a lower temperature than the plane, the heat energy is being converted into work without such a side effect, and although conservation of energy is not violated, the law of entropy is, and choice D is correct.

28. C: If the 200 kg barrel has an acceleration of 0.13 m/s², the net force on the barrel is $\sum F = ma =$ $(200\ kg)(0.13\ m/s^2) = 26\ N$. Since Jim is exerting a force of 320 N, there must be a force working against him with a magnitude of 320 N - 26 N = 294 N.

29. D: The force binding quarks into protons, and nucleons into nuclei, is the strong nuclear force. Electrons are attracted to protons by the electromagnetic force. However, it is the weak nuclear force, choice D that governs the decay of subatomic particles, for example the decay of a neutron into a proton, an electron, and a neutrino.

30. A: The energy released by the reaction cannot have been created out of nothing, but has to have come from somewhere or something. In this case, some of the mass of the particles is converted into energy, according to the mass-energy equivalence relation, $E=mc^2$. Since some mass is therefore lost, the total mass before the reaction (the total mass of the hydrogen nuclei) must be slightly larger than the total mass after the reaction (the mass of the helium nucleus); this is expressed in choice A:

31. C: To find the magnitude of the electromagnetic force use Coulomb's Law, $F = \frac{kq_1q_2}{r^2}$. Clearly, the masses do not actually enter into this equation, and they are not needed here. The charge of a $\frac{(8.99\times10^9 \text{ N·m}^2/\text{C}^2)(-1.6\times10^{-19}\text{ C})(1.6\times10^{-19}\text{ C})}{(1\times10^{-4}\text{ m})^2} = -2.3 \times 10^{-20}$ N. (Since we are asked for the magnitude of the force, we can ignore the negative sign.)

32. C: To find the speed of the torpedo relative to the island, the speed of the submarine relative to the island must be added to the speed of the torpedo relative to the submarine. However, since these velocities are not in the same direction, they must be added as *vectors*:

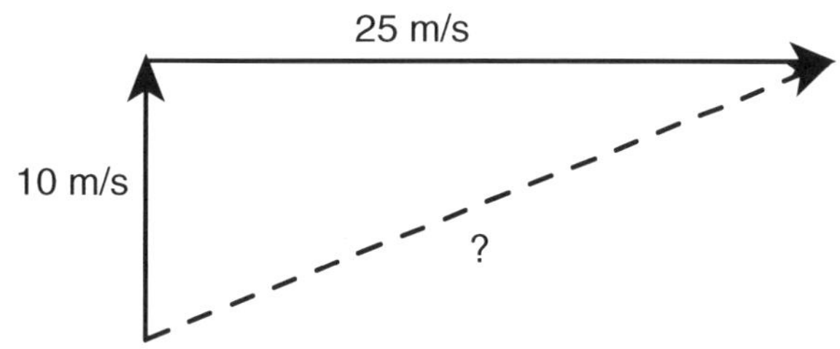

The missing velocity can be found by using the Pythagorean theorem: $x = \sqrt{(10\text{ m/s})^2 + (25\text{ m/s})^2}$

≈ 27 m/s.

33. B: Refraction is governed by Snell's law, $n_1 \sin\theta_1 = n_2 \sin\theta_2$. If n_1 is defined to be the index of refraction of air, and n_2 the index of refraction of amber, Snell's law yields $n_1 \sin 32° = n_2 \sin 20°$. Solving for n_2 using the fact the index of refraction of air is very close to 1 yields $n_2 = \sin 32° / \sin 20° = 1.55$. Note these calculations must be performed in degree mode rather than radian.

34. D: The problem does not specify in what reference frame the speed of the suitcase should be measured. As such, the problem does not have a unique answer. Relative to the man the speed of the suitcase is 0 m/s; to the bus it is 1 m/s; to the street, it is 9 m/s. Since not enough information is provided, D is the best choice.

35. 163.3 m/s: If the rockets are identical and have the same efficiency, the same amount of energy goes into propelling each rocket. The changes in their mechanical energies should be equal. Since their gravitational potential energies do not change, their final kinetic energies must be equal. The first rocket has a kinetic energy of $\frac{1}{2}mv^2 = \frac{1}{2}(1000\text{ kg})(200\text{ m/s})^2 = 2.00\times10^7$ J. Equating this energy to that of the second rocket yields $\frac{1}{2}(1500\text{ kg})v_2^2 = 2.00\times10^7$ J. Solving for v_2 yields a speed of 163.3 m/s.

36. A: X-rays have a short wavelength (several orders of magnitude shorter than the wavelength of visible light), which rules out choices B and D: Choice C is true – photons with a shorter wavelength *do* have higher energies – but does not explain why x-rays are used in medical imaging. (If anything, the higher energy would seem to be a *dis*advantage for medical imaging, since it would mean a greater chance of tissue damage.) Only choice A accurately explains why x-rays are used in medical imaging.

37. D: When two quantities are multiplied or divided, the squares of their relative errors add. That is, if $Z = XY$, $\left(\frac{\Delta Z}{Z}\right)^2 = \left(\frac{\Delta X}{X}\right)^2 + \left(\frac{\Delta Y}{Y}\right)^2$. Absolute error for a measuring device is considered to be one half of the smallest unit that it can measure. In this case, since the meter stick measures to the nearest millimeter, it may be off by as much as half a millimeter. Since the stopwatch measures to the nearest 0.01 seconds, it may be off by as much as 0.005 seconds. Plugging these values into the equation yields $\left(\frac{\Delta v}{v}\right)^2 = \left(\frac{0.0005\text{ m}}{1\text{ m}}\right)^2 + \left(\frac{0.005\text{ s}}{5\text{ s}}\right)^2 = 1.25 \times 10^{-6}$. To solve for Δv, take the square root of both sides and multiply by v: $\Delta v = 0.000224$. This narrows the choice to A and D. When two quantities are multiplied or divided, the number of significant figures in the result is equal to the least number of significant figures in each quantity. In this case, the time measurement has three; therefore, answer D is the correct choice.

38. C: In 1968, Sheldon Glashow, Abdus Salam, and Steven Weinberg developed a theory that united electricity and the weak nuclear force as manifestations of a unified electroweak interaction. The strong nuclear force was later coordinated with the electroweak interaction in the standard model of particle physics. Physicists have yet to discover a fully satisfactory theory that combines the gravitational force with the other three. Choice C is correct.

39. D: The work done on an object is equal to its total change in energy, including the change in potential energy. If an object's potential energy increases, then the work done is greater than the change in the kinetic energy (since $\Delta KE + \Delta PE > \Delta KE$). If the object's potential energy decreases, then the work done is less than the change in the kinetic energy (since $\Delta KE + \Delta PE < \Delta KE$). If only the kinetic energy changes, then the work done is equal to the change in kinetic energy. Since no further information is given, D is the correct choice.

40. B: While objects could be targeted by singular photons, this does not relate to the microscope's function. The uncertainty principle, if anything, would prevent knowledge of exact contours, and quantum entanglement refers to objects expressible by the same wavefunction and is not applicable to the observer. Electron microscopes instead work because the electron beam "illuminates" the observed object in a manner analogous to the way visible light illuminates objects in an optical microscope; that is, by reflecting from and being diffracted by the objects, and B is correct. The reason that electron microscopes can yield much higher magnifications is because electrons have a much smaller wavelength than visible light.

41. B: Choice D would violate the law of conservation of energy. If the chemicals heat up, their temperatures increase, and their kinetic energies therefore increase, so energy could not have been obtained from kinetic energy, so choice A is incorrect. Nor do chemical reactions typically involve absorption of heat from the environment as stated by choice C: Choice B correctly describes the situation: chemical bonds contain some amount of potential energy, which may be released in certain chemical reactions.

42. A: Acceleration is equal to change in velocity, and can be obtained by determining the velocity of the cart at two points along the track. The best choice is to find the velocity between the first two photogates and between the last two photogates. For each of these, we can use $v = \Delta x/\Delta t$: between the first two photogates, v_1 = 0.100 m / (0.079 s - 0 s) = 1.27 m/s, and between the second two, v_2 = 0.100 m / (0.586 s - 0.551 s) = 2.86 m/s. From here, there are at least two approaches to get an approximate answer for the acceleration, either the formula $v_2^2 = v_1^2+2ax$, solved for a to get a = ((2.86 m/s)^2 - (1.27 m/s)^2)/2(1.00 m) = 3.3 m/s^2, or the formula $v_2 = v_1 + at$, setting t equal to the time it takes to pass from the second to the third photogate (0.551 s - 0.079 s = 0.472 s) and solving for a to get a = (2.86 m/s - 1.27 m/s)/(0.472 s) = 3.4 m/s^2. While these answers don't exactly match any of the given choices, they are clearly closest to choice A.

Although this approximate result is good enough to select the correct choice, we can get a more accurate answer by taking into account that the velocities we calculated aren't really the velocities at the point the cart passes the second and third photogates; they are respectively the average velocity between the first and second photogates, and the average velocity between the third and fourth. These average velocities, however, are equal to the instantaneous velocities at the halfway point (with respect to time, not distance) of each interval. The halfway point of the first interval is the time t_1 = (0 s + 0.079 s)/2 = 0.0395 s, and for the second interval, t_2 = (0.551 s + 0.586 s)/2 = 0.5685 s. We can then use t = 0.569 s – 0.040 s = 0.0529 s, and a = (0.286 m/s – 0.127 m/s)/(0.529 s) = 3.0 m/s^2.

43. A: The specific heat of a substance depends mainly on the number of degrees of freedom of its molecules. All else being equal, a diatomic molecule tends to have more degrees of freedom, and hence a higher specific heat, than a monatomic molecule. A molecule with three atoms, such as ozone, should tend to have still more degrees of freedom, and a still higher specific heat. Therefore, we would expect monatomic oxygen to have a lower specific heat than either diatomic oxygen or ozone; this is expressed by choice A.

44. D: Voltages are equal in parallel and sum in series. An arrangement of identical batteries placed in parallel yields only the voltage of one battery. (This arrangement would, however, have a larger capacity, and hence would last longer than a single battery.) An array of identical batteries placed in series yield the total voltage of all the batteries. Arrangement A shows four batteries in parallel, yields the voltage of a single battery. Arrangement B shows two batteries in series, in parallel with another two batteries in series, and arrangement C shows the opposite, with two batteries in parallel, in series with another two in parallel. Each pair of batteries in series yields the voltage of two batteries, but only the voltage of one pair when put in parallel. Each pair of batteries in parallel yields the voltage of a single battery; two such pairs put in series yields the voltage of two batteries. All the batteries in arrangement D are in series, so arrangement D yields the voltage of four batteries, the highest of the four choices.

45. 546.4 Hz: The general equation for the Doppler frequency is $f = \frac{(v+v_r)}{(v+v_s)} f_0$, where v is the velocity of the wave through the medium (in this case, the speed of sound), and v_r and v_s are respectively the speed of the receiver and of the source relative to the medium. In this case, the receiver (the person standing in front of the train) is stationary relative to the medium (the air), so $v_r = 0$. Since the source is moving toward the receiver, v_s is negative. That yields $f = \frac{(340\text{ m/s})}{(340\text{ m/s}-60\text{ m/s})} 450\text{ Hz} = 546.4\ Hz$.

46. D: An electric motor works because the magnetic field generated by the magnet produces a force on the current-carrying coil, causing it to rotate. However, when the coil is aligned parallel to the field, the force will vanish, and the rotation will stop. Even if the coil's rotational momentum makes it overshoot this position a little, the magnetic force will tend to rotate it back the other way. To prevent this and make the coil continue rotating, the ends of the coil are attached to a commutator that comes into contact with the power source through stationary brushes. When the coil's rotation passes the halfway point, the brushes will pass the gap in the commutator, and each brush will now be in contact with the opposite end of the coil, causing the current in the coil to reverse direction, which means the magnetic force will again be in such a direction as to continue causing rotation in the same direction. For this to work, it is essential that the power source be connected to the brushes, not to the commutator or to the coil directly. (Connecting the power source to the magnet would not do anything.) D is correct.

47. D: Twice the initial wavelength would be 400 nm. This light would have a frequency of $f = c / \lambda$ = (3×10^8 m/s) / (4×10^{-7} m) = 7.5×10^{14} Hz. This is below the threshold frequency of 1.11×10^{15} Hz, so regardless of the light's intensity no electrons will be ejected, and no current will be produced.

48. C: The passengers are thrown forward because of their inertia; in the absence of an external force, they tend to preserve their state of motion (in this case, in the direction of the car's movement), even if the car around them stops. (Of course, they will eventually encounter external forces that will stop them, such as the tension in their seatbelts.) Although this manifests as a short continuation of existing kinetic energy, the energy conservation law is not governing the phenomenon, nor certainly are entropic or relativistic laws. Choice C is correct.

49. B: Since no information is given about how elastic the collision was, it is safest to avoid appealing to conservation of kinetic energy, but this problem can be solved using conservation of momentum. Before the collision, the total momentum is (100 kg)(4.0 m/s) = 400 kg·m/s. (The second sled's initial velocity is zero, so it has no momentum.) After the collision, the first sled's momentum is (100 kg)(1.0 m/s) = 100 kg·m/s. Since the total momentum is conserved, the second sled's momentum must then be 400 kg·m/s – 100 kg·m/s = 300 kg·m/s, and its speed must be (300 kg·m/s) / (80 kg) = 3.8 m/s.

50. C: An ammeter has a very low resistance, the better to cause current to flow through it freely. Placing an ammeter in parallel with another circuit element (as in choices A and D) will cause almost all the current to go through the ammeter instead of the circuit element, essentially creating a short circuit, leading to, at best inaccurate readings. It should therefore always be placed in series with the element through which the current is being measured. A voltmeter, on the other hand, has a very high resistance and should always be placed in parallel with the element across which the voltage is being measured. Placing a voltmeter in series with another circuit element (as in choices B and D) will lead to an essentially open circuit and, again, at best give inaccurate readings. The only diagram that correctly shows the ammeter in series and the voltmeter in parallel is choice C.

Regents Practice Test #2

1. A particle in a ring-shaped particle accelerator travels at a high constant speed along a circular path. In what direction is the particle's acceleration?

a. In the same direction as its motion
b. At constant speed, its acceleration is zero
c. Toward the center of the circle
d. Away from the center of the circle

2. In what units is impulse measured?

a. J
b. N
c. m/s^2
d. kg·m/s

3. The graph below shows the behavior over time of a particular point of the medium in which a wave is traveling. To what kind of wave does the graph most likely correspond?

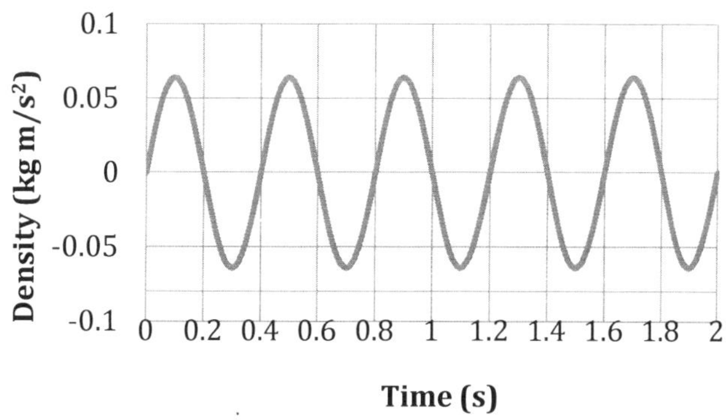

a. A transverse wave
b. A longitudinal wave
c. An electromagnetic wave
d. A water wave

4. Two small conductive spheres each carry a charge of $+5.0\times10^{-5}$ C: How far apart should the spheres be in order that the force between them is equal to 140 N?

a. 1.8 cm
b. 16 cm
c. 40 cm
d. 1.9 m

5. On a frictionless pool table, a cue ball with a mass of 0.18 kg collides with a stationary ball with a mass of 0.16 kg. The collision is perfectly elastic. After the collision, the cue ball's speed is 0.75 m/s. What was its speed before the collision, in m/s? Record and bubble in your answer to the nearest tenth on the answer document.

6. A student calculates the net external force on an object equals zero, and concludes the object is motionless. What is wrong with his reasoning?

a. Zero net external force means only that acceleration is zero
b. It is impossible for the net external force to be zero; he must have miscalculated
c. The student forgot to take into account the reaction forces
d. Nothing is wrong; his reasoning is correct

7. The simple generator shown below works because the rotation of the magnetic rotor produces a changing magnetic field that induces a voltage and current in the surrounding wire coil.

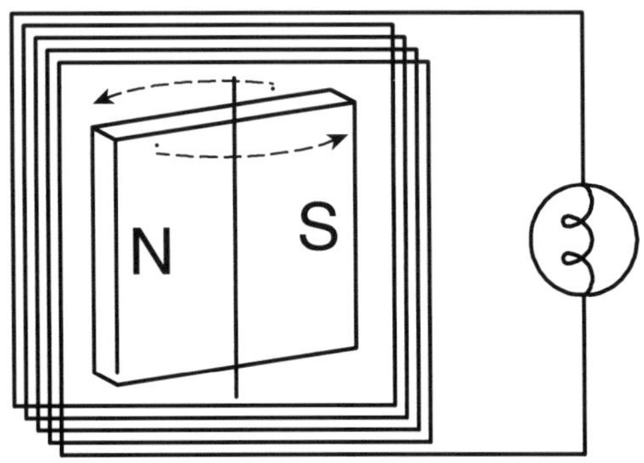

Which of the following best describes the behavior of the current over time?

a. Increasing
b. Decreasing
c. Alternating
d. Constant

8. In which of the following materials would you expect sound waves to travel most rapidly?

a. Air
b. Aluminum
c. Rubber
d. Water

9. The graph below shows the velocity of a go-cart over time:

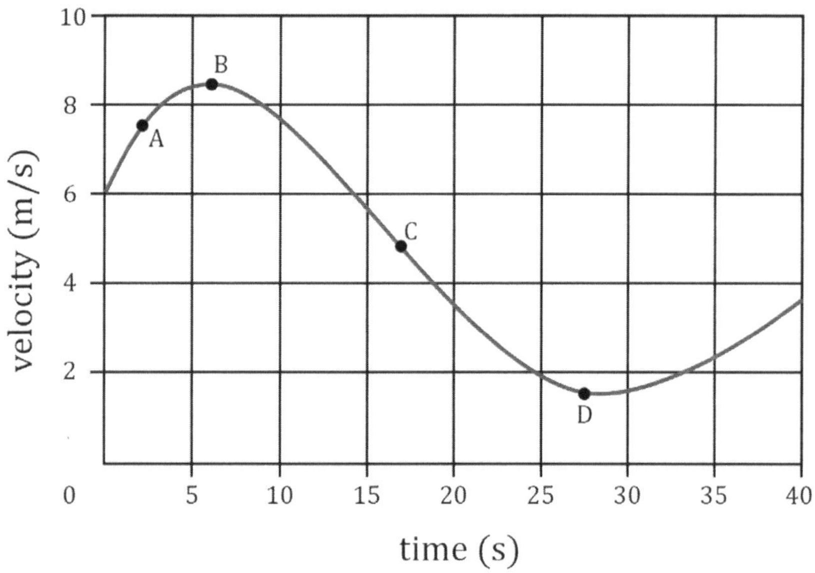

At which of the labeled points on the graph is the go-cart's acceleration greatest?

a. Point A
b. Point B
c. Point C
d. Point D

10. Which of the following processes violates the law of entropy?

a. A lake freezing over in winter
b. The construction of a building
c. The development of a living being
d. None of the above

11. Which of the following scientists famously contributed to the study of the weak nuclear force?

a. Albert Einstein
b. Enrico Fermi
c. Brian Greene
d. Stephen Hawking

12. Which of the following free-body force diagrams could correspond to a stationary object?

a.

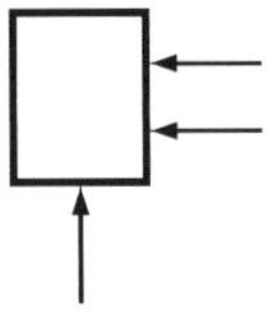

b.

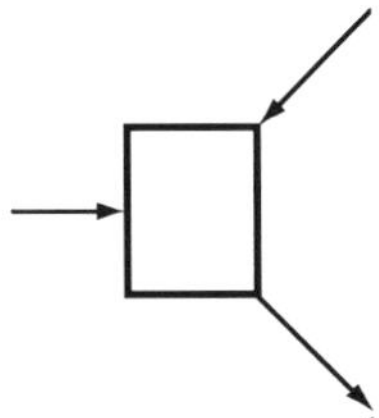

c.

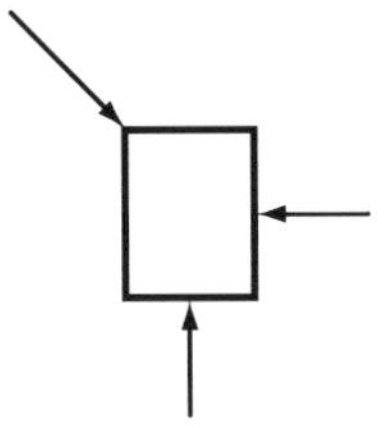

d.

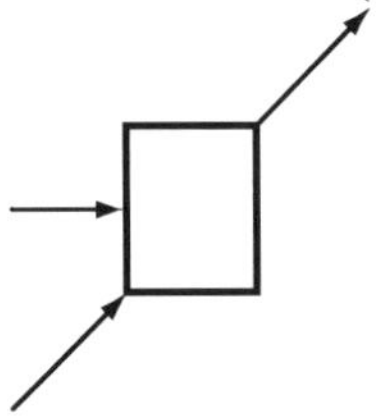

13. One atom of uranium-235 undergoes nuclear fission, releasing an energy of 3.24×10^{-11} J. What is the difference between the combined mass of the products of the fission reaction and the mass of the original uranium atom?

a. 1.17×10^{-38} kg
b. 2.92×10^{-30} kg
c. 3.50×10^{-30} kg
d. 3.60×10^{-28} kg

14. A man begins to push a heavy box initially at rest across a flat concrete floor. When he is done, he has moved the box (now at rest again) eight meters. What has happened to the energy the man used to push the box?

a. It was lost to heat through friction and air resistance
b. It went to increase the potential energy of the box
c. It went to increase the potential energy of the man
d. It was converted into mass

15. Two asteroids have masses of 2.12×10^{18} kg and 8.78×10^{17} kg. The distance between the centers of the two asteroids is 5.00×10^{8} km. What is the magnitude of the gravitational force that each asteroid exerts on the other? Record and bubble in your answer to the nearest Newton on the answer document.

16. A train moves east along a level track at a speed of 11 m/s. A boy onboard the train runs toward the back of the train at a speed (relative to the train) of 2 m/s. While running, he throws a ball ahead of himself, at a speed (relative to the boy) of 4 m/s. From what frame of reference does the ball have the highest speed?

a. The reference frame of the boy
b. The reference frame of the ball
c. The reference frame of the train
d. The reference frame of the ground outside the train

17. Which of the following best explains why radiation therapy is used to treat cancer?

a. The strong electromagnetic forces in the radiation pull cancer cells apart
b. The waves of the radiation have just the right frequency to destructively interfere with the cancer cells
c. The high frequency of the radiation causes cancer cells to vibrate so fast they shake themselves apart
d. The high-energy photons or charged particles of the radiation impact and damage vital molecules in the cancer cells, killing them

18. A Smith & Wesson revolver has a mass of 2.00 kg. It fires a bullet with a velocity of 600 m/s. When the gun fires the bullet, however, recoil kicks the gun in the opposite direction. If the bullet's mass is 23 grams, what is the velocity with which the gun is knocked backward by recoil?

a. 6.9 m/s
b. 14 m/s
c. 64 m/s
d. 600 m/s

19. If an object moves from one point to another, which of the following most accurately describes the relative magnitudes of its displacement and the total distance it traveled?

a. The total distance is always less than or equal to the displacement
b. The total distance is always greater than or equal to the displacement
c. The total displacement may be greater than, less than, or equal to the displacement
d. The total distance and the displacement are always equal

20. In the circuit diagrammed below, what is the current through the 100 Ω resistor?

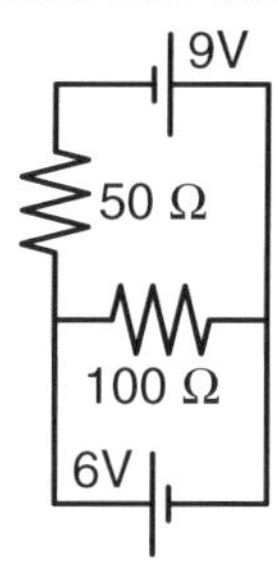

a. 60 mA
b. 300 mA
c. 3.30 A
d. 16.7 A

21. Which of the following best describes how you could find the resonant frequency of a model bridge?

a. Divide the speed of sound in air by half the bridge's width
b. Divide the speed of sound in air by half the bridge's length
c. Shake the bridge at various frequencies and record when the amplitude of vibration is maximized
d. Shake the bridge at various frequencies and record when the amplitude of vibration is minimized

22. A student set up a series of photogates along a track at 10-centimeter intervals, synchronized and set to record the time at which an object passed through them. He then slid a glider along the track, intending to measure its (negative) acceleration and thereby calculate the coefficient of friction. Unfortunately, he learned after performing the experiment that one of the photogates used was defective. The following data was obtained from the experiment.

	Photogate 1	Photogate 2	Photogate 3	Photogate 4	Photogate 5	Photogate 6
Time	0 s	0.16 s	0.22 s	0.56 s	0.85 s	1.43 s

Based on this data, which photogate is most likely to have been defective?

a. Photogate 2
b. Photogate 3
c. Photogate 4
d. Photogate 5

23. Which of the following is an example of heat transfer through convection?

a. A microwave cooking food
b. A pancake cooking on an electric burner
c. A planet heated by the sun
d. A coastline heated by a warm ocean current

24. Which scientist or natural philosopher first demonstrated all objects are accelerated by gravity at the same rate?

a. Henry Cavendish
b. Galileo Galilei
c. Johannes Kepler
d. Isaac Newton

25. In one minute, the sound of the "song" of a particular humpback whale travels 93.60 kilometers. One particular note of the song has a wavelength of 3.10 m. What is the frequency of this note? Record and bubble in your answer to the nearest Hertz on the answer document.

26. A wagon is initially moving horizontally with a velocity of 2.0 m/s. It then goes down a hill 3.0 meters high. At the bottom of the hill, it is moving with a velocity of 9.0 m/s. Which of the following can be concluded from this?

a. The wagon's total energy was conserved; there no outside forces acted on it.
b. Some outside force was supplying energy to the wagon (such as an engine or something pushing it).
c. Some outside force was taking energy away from the wagon (such as friction or air resistance).
d. The wagon is massless.

27. A boy whirls a ball on a string, spinning it in a circle 1.5 meters in diameter. The ball completes two revolutions every second. If the mass of the ball is 80 grams, what is the tension in the string?

a. 0.59 N
b. 1.2 N
c. 9.5 N
d. 19 N

28. One popular trick is to rub a balloon on someone's hair and then place it against a wall, where the balloon will stay stuck in place. Which of the following best describes why this happens?

a. Rubbing the balloon on the hair heats it up and slightly melts part of it; in contact with the wall, it resolidifies and sticks
b. Rubbing the balloon on the hair magnetizes it, like rubbing a needle on a magnet. It is magnetically attracted to the wall
c. Rubbing the balloon on the hair smooths out a part of the balloon, making it so perfectly flat that it sticks like a suction cup
d. Rubbing the balloon on the hair gives it a slight negative electric charge. It is electrostatically attracted to positively charged particles in the wall.

29. Which of the following elements would you expect to have the most lines in its emission spectrum?

a. Carbon
b. Helium
c. Hydrogen
d. Iron

30. Which of the following is always true of action-reaction force pairs?

a. The forces in such pairs have the same magnitude
b. The forces in such pairs have the same direction
c. The forces in such pairs act on the same object
d. The forces in such pairs cancel each other, producing no change in the system

31. A 100-gram weight hangs motionless from a massless spring. If the weight is pulled down 40 centimeters from this equilibrium position, stretching the spring, what other information is needed to calculate the amount of work done on the spring?

a. The length of the spring when no mass is hung from it
b. The elastic potential energy of the stretched spring
c. The time it took to pull the weight down
d. None; there is already enough information to conclude no work was done on the spring

32. The following table shows the dimensions and measured resistances of cylinders made from four different alloys.

	Length (mm)	Radius (mm)	Resistance (Ω)
Alloy 1	10.0	4.0	5.27×10^{-6}
Alloy 2	20.0	3.0	3.57×10^{-5}
Alloy 3	40.0	2.0	6.30×10^{-5}
Alloy 4	30.0	1.0	5.95×10^{-4}

Based on this data, which material is the best conductor?

a. Alloy 1
b. Alloy 2
c. Alloy 3
d. Alloy 4

33. Which of the following correctly describes an image in a plane mirror?

a. Real and upright
b. Real and inverted
c. Virtual and upright
d. Virtual and inverted

34. If all other quantities are held constant, increasing the temperature of a gas also increases its pressure. Which of the following best explains why this is the case?

a. Increasing the temperature of the gas increases the potential energy of its molecules. This increases the molecules' effective size, causing them to press more against other objects and surfaces
b. Increasing the temperature of the gas increases the potential energy of its molecules. This potential energy is released as pressure when they hit a surface
c. Increasing the temperature of the gas increases the kinetic energy of its molecules. This decreases their potential energy, which is inversely proportional to pressure
d. Increasing the temperature of the gas increases the kinetic energy of its molecules. This means they hit surfaces with a greater force, which is proportional to pressure

35. A dog spends several minutes trotting back and forth along a one-dimensional straight pathway. The graph below shows the dog's position as a function of time.

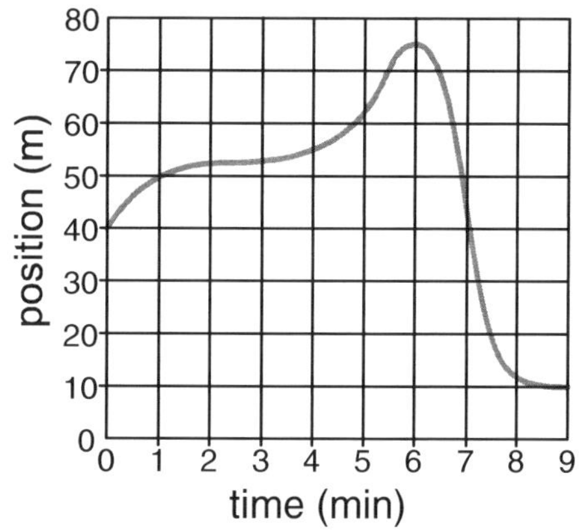

What is the dog's overall average speed, in meters per second? Record and bubble in your answer to the nearest thousandth on the answer document.

36. Through the photoelectric effect, electrons are emitted from materials exposed to certain frequencies of electromagnetic radiation. Which of the following facts about the photoelectric effect gives the most direct evidence for the dual nature of light?

a. The more intense the incident light, the more electrons are emitted
b. No electrons are emitted when the frequency of the incident light is below a certain threshold
c. If the incident light is polarized, most of the electrons are emitted in the direction of polarization
d. Less than a nanosecond elapses between the incidence of the light and the emission of the electron

37. Which of the following would halve the gravitational force between two objects?

a. Halving the mass of one of the objects
b. Halving the mass of both objects
c. Doubling the distance between the objects
d. Quadrupling the distance between the objects (multiplying it by four)

38. Through what method of heat transfer would an object freely floating in outer space lose most of its heat energy?

a. Conduction
b. Convection
c. Radiation
d. None of the above; an object floating in space would retain its heat indefinitely

39. The acceleration of gravity on the surface of the moon is 1.62 m/s^2. If a man weighs 800 N on the Earth, how much would he weigh on the moon?

a. 132 N
b. 493 N
c. 4840 N
d. Because the moon orbits the Earth, on the moon a man would be weightless

40. Which of the following most closely resembles the typical pattern formed by monochromatic light diffracted through a single vertical slit?

a. 

b. 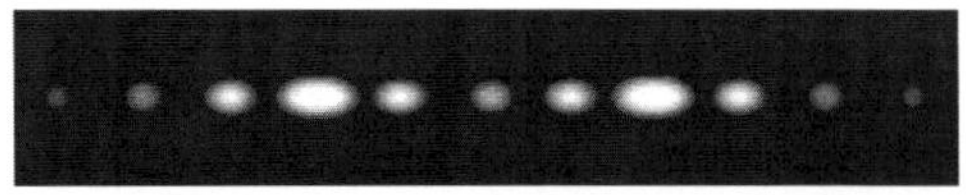

c. 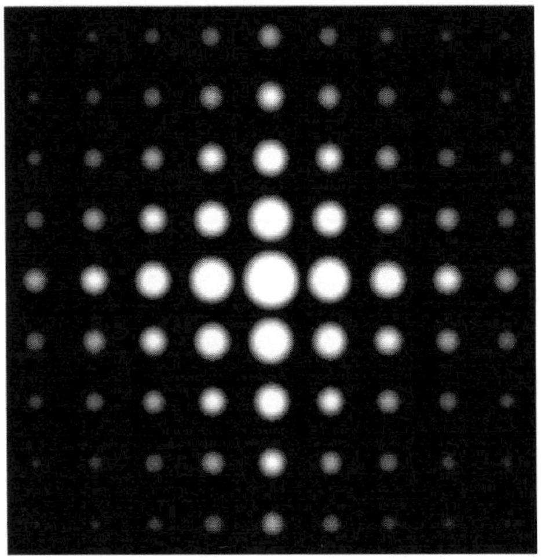

d. 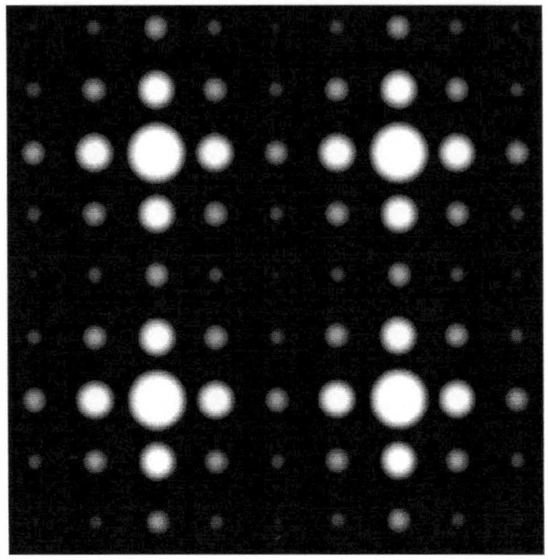

41. What nineteenth-century scientist famously developed a set of equations describing the interactions between electrical and magnetic fields and forces, and at the same time established that electromagnetic waves travel at the speed of light?

a. André-Marie Ampère
b. Charles-Augustin de Coulomb
c. Michael Faraday
d. James Clerk Maxwell

42. An archer fires an arrow and hits a target 500 meters away over level ground (the arrow's final height above the ground is the same as its initial height). If the arrow's initial speed was 80 m/s, what was the angle above the horizontal of the arrow's initial velocity?

a. 0°
b. 11°
c. 25°
d. 34°

43. A ride at an amusement park consists of twelve "rocket cars" that move in a circle with a radius of six meters, at their top speed taking three seconds to complete a full rotation. Each car has a mass of 500 kg. What is the total kinetic energy of the ride, when the cars are moving at top speed? (Assume that the mass of the rods supporting the rockets is negligible, and that the cars are small enough relative to the radius of their path to be treated as point masses.)

a. 0 J
b. 3.9×10^4 J
c. 7.5×10^4 J
d. 4.8×10^5 J

44. "Ultrasound" is often used in medical applications to image the interior of the human body, for example, to look at a developing fetus inside a womb. Which of the following properties of ultrasound gives it its name?

a. It has a very high amplitude
b. It has a very high frequency
c. It has a very high velocity
d. It has a very large wavelength

45. Each of the resistors in the part of a circuit shown below has a resistance of 120 Ω. What is the effective resistance of the entire arrangement? Record and bubble in your answer to the nearest tenth of an ohm on the answer document.

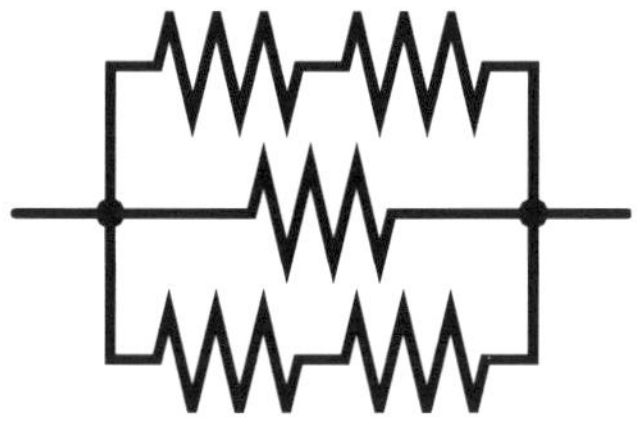

46. A ship accelerates for 30 seconds at a constant, positive rate. Which of the following velocities should be greatest?

a. The average velocity
b. The instantaneous velocity at $t = 0$ s
c. The instantaneous velocity at $t = 15$ s
d. The instantaneous velocity at $t = 30$ s

47. A boy swings on a rope over a lake. When he steps off of the ledge to start his swing, he is 2.0 meters above the lake surface. At the bottom of the swing, just as he lets go of the rope, he is 0.5 meters above the surface. What is the boy's horizontal speed at the bottom of the swing?

a. 5.4 m/s
b. 6.3 m/s
c. 7.7 m/s
d. 8.9 m/s

48. The graph below displays the displacement from equilibrium over time of a point on a vibrating string.

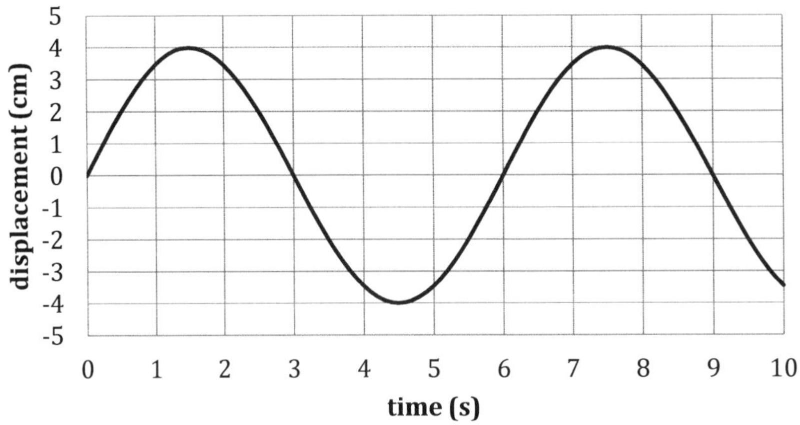

What is the amplitude of the vibration?

a. 3 s
b. 4 cm
c. 6 s
d. 8 cm

49. What force is responsible for holding together the protons and neutrons in an atomic nucleus?

a. Gravitational force
b. Electromagnetic force
c. The weak nuclear force
d. The strong nuclear force

50. A car slows at a constant rate and comes to a stop over a distance of 40 m. If the car's initial velocity was 20 m/s, what was the magnitude of its acceleration?

a. 5 m/s^2
b. 10 m/s^2
c. 15 m/s^2
d. 20 m/s^2

Answer Key and Explanations for Test #2

1. C: The acceleration of an object in uniform circular motion is always toward the center of the circle. The object's inertia tends to keep it moving a tangential path that carries it away from the center of the circle. An acceleration of the appropriate magnitude directed toward the center of the circle can balance that tendency and keep the object's distance from the center of the circle constant. C is correct.

2. D: Impulse is equal to change in momentum; it has the same units as momentum. Momentum is equal to mass times velocity; it has the units of mass (kg) times the units of velocity (m/s). This is represented in choice D.

3. B: The key point to notice here is that the y-axis is measuring density. In a transverse mechanical wave (including water waves, though they also involve some oscillation parallel to the direction of motion), it is the displacement from equilibrium of a point in the medium of propagation that varies with time. In an electromagnetic wave, it is the electric and magnetic fields, not the density of the medium, that vary. Only in a longitudinal wave do compressions and expansions of the particles of the medium cause the density of the medium to oscillate, and B is correct.

4. C: The formula for the force between two charged bodies is Coulomb's law, $= \frac{kq_1q_2}{r^2}$.

Solving for r, we get $r = \sqrt{\frac{kq_1q_2}{F}}$.

Given values readily yield a value for r of $r = \sqrt{(9.0 \times 10^9 \text{ N·m}^2/\text{C}^2)(5.0 \times 10^{-5} \text{ C})^2/(140 \text{ N})}$

$= 0.40$ m

$= 40$ cm.

5. 12.8 m/s: Two conservation laws apply here: the law of conservation of momentum and the law of conservation of energy (since the collision was perfectly elastic). There are two unknowns, the initial velocity v_{1i} of the cue ball, and the final velocity v_{2f} of the other ball, so the two equations derived from these conservation laws can be used to solve for the unknowns. A much simpler approach is to recall the equations for perfectly elastic collisions. In particular, if v_{2i} is zero, as is the case here, since the second ball is initially stationary, then $v_{1f} = v_{1i}\frac{m_1-m_2}{m_1+m_2}$ and $v_{2f} = v_{1i}\frac{2m_1}{m_1+m_2}$.

Since v_{2f} is not known, the second equation is not useful here, but the first can be solved for v_{1i} to get $v_{1i} = v_{1f}\frac{m_1+m_2}{m_1-m_2} = (0.75 \text{ m/s})\frac{0.18 \text{ kg}+0.16 \text{ kg}}{0.18 \text{ kg}-0.16 \text{ kg}} = 12.8 \text{ m/s}$.

If one doesn't remember the above equation, it can in fact be obtained from the equations that result when the conservation laws are applied, if one doesn't mind some algebraic legwork. A derivation of the equation used above follows.

Start with conservation of momentum, $m_1v_{1i} + m_2v_{2i} = m_1v_{1f} + m_2v_{2f}$. Solve for $v2f$ using the fact $v2i = 0$ to obtain $v_{2f} = \frac{m_1v_{1i}-m_1v_{1f}}{m_2}$. Although it may seem strange to solve for v_{2f}, it is only to facilitate setting two expressions equal to solve for v_{1i}.

Now consider conservation of kinetic energy, $\frac{1}{2}m_1v_{1i}^2 + \frac{1}{2}m_2v_{2i}^2 = \frac{1}{2}m_1v_{1f}^2 + \frac{1}{2}m_2v_{2f}^2$. Again using the fact $v2\mathrm{i} = 0$, solve for $v2\mathrm{f}2$ to obtain $v_{2f}^2 = \frac{m_1v_{1i}^2 - m_1v_{1f}^2}{m_2}$. Square the expression obtained for $v2\mathrm{f}$ from conservation of momentum, and set it equal to that obtained for $v2\mathrm{f}2$ from kinetic energy conservation to obtain $\left(\frac{m_1v_{1i} - m_1v_{1f}}{m_2}\right)^2 = \frac{m_1v_{1i}^2 - m_1v_{1f}^2}{m_2}$. Chase through the algebra and group like terms in $v1\mathrm{i}$ to obtain $v_{1i}^2(m_1^2 - m_1m_2) - v_{1i}(2m_1^2v_{1f}) + (v_{1f}^2[m_1^2 + m_1m_2]) = 0$, where parentheses are used to set the coefficients apart. Apply the quadratic formula to obtain $v_{1i} = \frac{(2m_1^2v_{1f}) \pm \sqrt{(2m_1^2v_{1f})^2 - 4(m_1^2 - m_1m_2)v_{1f}^2(m_1^2 + m_1m_2)}}{2(m_1^2 - m_1m_2)}$. Chase through the algebra again to obtain $v_{1i} = v_{1f}\left(\frac{m_1 \pm m_2}{m_1 - m_2}\right)$. Clearly, subtraction in the numerator yields $v_{1i} = v_{1f}$, a result that is not meaningful here, as it corresponds to the second ball remaining stationary! Addition in the numerator yields the exact expression for v1i used above to calculate the answer of 12.8 m/s.

6. A: If there is zero net external force on an object (which, contrary to choice B, is certainly possible), then the object's acceleration is zero, which means its velocity is constant. However, the velocity could be zero *or* any other non-zero constant; this is the error in the student's reasoning described in choice A: The reaction forces mentioned in choice C are irrelevant, because they act on different objects and will not affect the net force on the object in question.

7. C: As depicted, this generator would produce an alternating current. As the magnetic rotor rotates the direction of its magnetic field will also rotate. When the magnetic field is perpendicular to the coil, the current has its maximum magnitude. After a quarter-rotation, however, the magnetic field will be parallel to the coil and no current will be induced. After another quarter-rotation, the magnetic field will again be perpendicular to the coil, but the magnetic field will be in the opposite direction; the current will again have its maximum magnitude, but will flow in the reverse direction. After another quarter-rotation, the magnetic field will again be parallel to the coil and the current equal to zero, and then with another quarter-rotation the cycle repeats. The only choice that describes this behavior is C.

8. B: The speed of sound, like the speed of other mechanical waves, depends on the density and the rigidity of the medium. The less dense and the more rigid a medium, the faster sound waves will travel through it. Aluminum is both less dense and more rigid than rubber or water, so we expect the speed of sound to be greater in aluminum than in either of these media. While aluminum is denser than air, it is much, much more rigid than air; in general, sound tends to travel faster through solids and liquids than through gases. We therefore expect the speed of sound to be greater in aluminum than in air as well, and B is the correct choice. (The approximate speed of sound in aluminum is over 6000 m/s, as opposed to about 1600 m/s in rubber, 1500 m/s in water, and 340 m/s in air. While different sources may list slightly different numbers, in all cases the speed of sound is much greater in aluminum than in the other media.)

9. A: Acceleration is equal to the slope of the graph of velocity versus time. At points B and D, the slope of the graph is zero, so the acceleration is zero. The slope of the graph is steeper at point A than at point C, so the magnitude of the acceleration is greater at A: (Additionally, at point C the slope, and therefore the acceleration, is negative, less than any non-negative value.) Therefore, of the four labeled points, the acceleration is greatest at point A.

10. D: The law of entropy states that the total entropy of a closed system cannot decrease. It does not preclude the entropy of *part* of the system decreasing, as long as the entropy of some other part of the system increases to compensate. This is exactly what is described in choices A, B, and C: Ice has less entropy than water, but when the pond freezes it releases heat, increasing the entropy of its surroundings. A building has less entropy than its raw materials, but the construction of a building requires work from machines and human workers, both of which produce energy by processing low-entropy fuels into energy and high-entropy waste products. While living things may have low entropy, it is by relying on external sources of energy which produce large increases in entropy elsewhere. For example, most food chains on Earth are ultimately based on energy from the sun, the entropy of which is constantly increasing as fusion reactions take place in its interior. Since in each case the total entropy of the system increases, none of these processes violates the law of entropy, and choice D is correct. Indeed, the law of entropy seems to be an immutable law that applies to all natural and artificial processes.

11. B: In 1933, Enrico Fermi developed a theory to explain beta decay through the interaction of four particles at one point, via the weak nuclear force. His theory was later refined by other physicists including Richard Feynman, Murray Gell-Mann, Robert Marshak, and George Sudarshan, who found a way to resolve certain mathematical problems with Fermi's theory. Still later, Sheldon Glashow, Abdus Salam, and Steven Weinberg connected the weak nuclear force to the electromagnetic force. While Einstein, Greene, and Hawking have contributed greatly in their respective fields, only Fermi focused on the weak force.

12. C: For an object to remain stationary, the net force on the object must be zero, which means that all forces acting on it must balance. In choice A, there are forces directed left and up, but no forces down or right to balance them. In choice B, there are forces directed both left and right, which may balance, but there are forces directed down and no forces directed up. Similarly, in choice D, there are forces directed to the right, but no forces directed to the left. Only in the diagram depicted in choice C is every force potentially balanced by another force with a component in the opposite direction.

13. D: To answer this problem, use the mass-energy equivalence relation, $E = mc^2$. Solving for m yields $m = E / c^2 = (3.24\times10^{-11}\text{ J}) / (3.00\times10^{-8}\text{ m/s})^2 = 3.60\times10^{-28}$ kg.

14. A: If the box is pushed along a flat surface, its altitude does not change, so its gravitational potential energy is constant. Since the box was at rest before and after its motion, its kinetic energy has not changed either, so it's total energy has not changed, and the work done on it must be equal to zero. The box's energy does not change, nor does the man's potential energy increase; if anything, his body's chemical potential energy decreases. (Mass-energy equivalence has no bearing on this situation, either.) However, as friction and air resistance act against the motion of the box, the energy is lost to heat and sound, and A is the correct answer. (If resistive forces like friction did not act, then after a single push the box would keep moving indefinitely. In this case, there would be work done on the box, because its kinetic energy would increase.)

15. 497 N: This problem is a straightforward application of the law of universal gravitation, $F = \frac{Gm_1m_2}{r^2}$. Recognizing the separation distance must be converted from kilometers, substituting values yields $F = \frac{(6.67\times10^{-11}\text{ N}\cdot\text{m}^2/\text{kg}^2)(2.12\times10^{18}\text{ kg})(8.78\times10^{17}\text{ kg})}{(5.00\times10^{11}\text{ m})^2} = 496.6 \approx 497\text{ N}.$

16. C: From the ball's own frame of reference, its speed is, of course, zero, so choice B is incorrect. From the boy's frame of reference, the ball's velocity is given as 4 m/s (towards the back of the train). From the frame of reference of the train, the ball's velocity is the boy's relative to the train, plus the ball's relative to the boy, or 2 m/s (towards the back) + 4 m/s (towards the back) = 6 m/s (towards the back). From the reference frame of the ground outside the train, the ball's velocity is the train's relative to the ground, plus the ball's relative to the train, or 11 m/s (towards the front) +

6 m/s (towards the back) = 11 m/s – 6 m/s = 5 m/s, where the subtraction indicates the velocities are in opposite directions. While the largest *velocity* may be +5 m/s (forward) rather than -6 m/s (backward), the greatest magnitude, that is, the greatest *speed*, is 6 m/s, the speed of the ball relative to the train. Choice C is correct.

17. D: Radiation therapy works because the high-energy photons or charged particles impact the DNA of the cancer cells, damaging it and harming the cells' ability to grow and reproduce. Of course, the radiation has the same effect on other cells, but healthy cells may have more resilient repair mechanisms for their DNA than cancer cells, making them somewhat less susceptible to radiation damage. Furthermore, the radiation is often applied in different beams that intersect at the site of the cancer cells, ensuring that the cancer cells get a much higher dosage than the surrounding healthy cells. Radiation therapy has nothing to do with destructively vibrating cancer cells or pulling them apart electromagnetically. Nor does it have to do with destructive wave interference: while cancer cells, like other particles and objects, may have associated DeBroglie wavelengths, these wavelengths are too small compared to those of the radiation used for interference to occur. The correct choice is D.

18. A: Recoil occurs due to conservation of momentum. Since the initial momenta of the gun and bullet are zero, the gun must have final momentum equal in magnitude and opposite in direction to that of the bullet (so that the total momentum is still zero). The momentum of the bullet is (0.023 kg)(600 m/s) = 13.8 kg·m/s (forward). This must be the magnitude of the gun's momentum, so that the gun's speed is (13.8 kg·m/s) / (2.00 kg) = 6.9 m/s.

19. B: The displacement is the distance between the start and end points. If the object traveled in a straight line between the points, its displacement and its total distance traveled are equal. If the object traveled in any other path, the total distance traveled is greater than the displacement. For example, if the object traveled in one complete circle, its displacement is zero (since its start and end points are the same), but the total distance traveled is equal to the circumference of the circle, which is greater than zero. The only choice that expresses this correctly is B.

20. A: There are three different values for the current through different parts of this circuit: the current through the 6 V battery, the current through the 100 Ω resistor, and the current through the 9 V battery and 50 Ω resistor. Kirchhoff's circuit laws can calculate each of these currents: the junction rule gives one relation between the currents, and applications of the loop rule yield two more; three equations to solve for three unknowns. However, applying Kirchhoff's loop rule to the bottom loop yields an equation that can be solved directly for the current through the 100 Ω resistor. Specifically, a clockwise loop yields 6 V – (100 Ω) $I = 0$, so that I = (6V / 100 Ω) = 60 mA, choice A: (Determining which direction this current flows through the 100 Ω resistor, left or right, requires solving the system of Kirchhoff equations, but for this problem, the magnitude is sufficient.)

21. C: An object's resonant frequency is the frequency at which it most easily vibrates. If an object is vibrated at its resonant frequency, the waves of the vibration will tend to constructively interfere, leading to very high amplitude of vibration. Although the resonant frequency may be related to the object's dimensions, other factors are also involved (such as mass) and measuring the width or length is insufficient. Furthermore, the resonant frequency of an object has nothing to do with the speed of sound in air, but with the speed of sound in the object itself. The most straightforward way, therefore, to determine an object's resonant frequency or frequencies is simply to vibrate it at different frequencies to determine at what frequency it vibrates most easily, that is, at what frequencies the amplitude is maximized, choice C.

22. B: There are a number of ways to answer this question, including determining which data point does not match a smooth curve connecting the points of a plot of distance traveled versus time, calculating the velocities between each pair of photogates to determine which do not follow the linear relationship expected from a constant acceleration, or calculating the acceleration to determine which data points do not match that calculation. However, examining the data more closely, the question can be answered more simply. The elapsed time between photogates 2 and 3 (0.22 s – 0.16 s = 0.08 s) is less than that between photogates 1 and 2 (0.16 s – 0 s = 0.16 s), which does not make sense: if the glider is slowing down, that is, if its acceleration is negative, the time intervals between successive pairs of photogates should increase. One of those three photogates must therefore be defective. Similarly, the elapsed time between photogates 3 and 4 (0.56 s – 0.22 s = 0.34 s) is greater than that between photogates 4 and 5 (0.84 s – 0.56 s = 0.28 s), which also does not make sense, for the same reason. One of these photogates must be defective, and the only photogate belonging to both sets is photogate 3; photogate 3 is defective.

23. D: Convection is a process through which heat is transferred within a fluid by the movement of molecules, including large-scale internal flow of the fluid itself. Of the given choices, only the coastline heated by the warm ocean current fits this description. Food is cooked in a microwave through radiation, and a pancake cooks primarily through conduction of heat from the burner to the pan to the pancake, and the sun heats planets through radiation of heat and energy through the intervening space. The correct answer is D.

24. B: Galileo demonstrated all objects are accelerated by gravity at the same rate at about the beginning of the seventeenth century. There is a famous story of his dropping objects from the Tower of Pisa as a part of this demonstration, although this may be a myth. Galileo's work laid the groundwork for Newton's discovery in the late seventeenth century of the law of universal gravitation. Kepler's work involved planetary orbits, and while Cavendish's experiment was the first to accurately determine the gravitational constant (on Earth), Galileo first demonstrated the universal acceleration rate of gravity, and the correct answer is B:

25. 503 Hz: If the sound travels 93.60 kilometers (9.360×10^4 meters) in one minute (60 seconds), then the speed of the sound wave is 9.360×10^4 m / 60 s = 1560 m/s, a typical value for the speed of sound in saltwater. The frequency of the sound wave can be obtained by using the relationship $v = f\lambda$: solving for f, this yields $f = v / \lambda$ = (1560 m/s) /(3.10 m) = 503.22 Hz ≈ 503 Hz. (The frequencies in whale song can range from 10 Hz to over 30 kHz!)

26. B: Initially, the wagon's kinetic energy is $\frac{1}{2}mv^2 = \frac{1}{2}m(2.0 \text{ m/s})^2 = (2.0 \text{ m}^2/\text{s}^2)\, m$. (Since the mass is unknown, the result must be expressed this way.) It also has potential energy of $mgh = m(9.8 \text{ m/s}^2)(3.0 \text{ m}) = (29.4 \text{ m}^2/\text{s}^2)\, m$, and its total initial energy is therefore $(2.0 \text{ m}^2/\text{s}^2)\, m + (29.4 \text{ m}^2/\text{s}^2)m = (31.4 \text{ m}^2/\text{s}^2)m$. After it goes down the hill, the wagon has no potential energy, but its kinetic energy is $\frac{1}{2}mv^2 = \frac{1}{2}m(9.0 \text{ m/s})^2 = (41 \text{ m}^2/\text{s}^2)\, m$. This is significantly larger than its initial energy (by a factor of 1.3), so there must have been something supplying the wagon with energy, and choice B is correct.

27. C: The tension in the string is equal to the centripetal force keeping the ball in circular motion, given by $F = mv^2/r$. Since the circumference of the circle of motion is $2\pi r = 2\pi(0.75 \text{ m}) = 4.71$ m, and the period of the motion is (1 s)/(2 rotations) = 0.5 s per rotation, the velocity is given by (4.71 m)/(0.5 s) = 9.42 m/s. The centripetal force, the tension in the string, is therefore $F = mv^2/r = (0.080 \text{ kg})(9.42 \text{ m/s})^2 / (0.75 \text{ m}) = 9.5$ N.

28. D: The electrons in human hair are relatively loosely bound, and tend to be lost to the balloon, the material of which has few electrons in the outer shells of its atoms. The balloon then becomes negatively charged. When placed in contact with the wall, that charge repels the negative particles in the wall resulting in a net positive charge at the surface, which attracts the negative charge on the balloon, keeping it in place. The same process causes the static electric charge that may be discharged with a spark if one brings one's finger close to a conductor after shuffling one's feet on some kinds of carpets.

29. D: Each line in an emission spectrum comes from photons emitted by electrons transitioning from a higher to a lower energy level. The more electrons an atom has, the greater the number of accessible energy levels, so that more different transition energies are possible and photons will be emitted with more different wavelengths, creating more lines in the spectrum. Hydrogen and helium, with only one and two electrons, respectively, are not likely to show many lines, since there are not many possible transitions. Carbon has six electrons, more than hydrogen and helium, but much fewer than iron, which has twenty-six, allowing many more possible electron transitions than any of the other three choices, and many more possible lines in its emission spectrum. D is correct.

30. A: The forces in action-reaction pairs have equal magnitude, but opposite direction, so B is incorrect. They act on different objects: if object A exerts a force on object B, then the reaction force is exerted by object B on object A, so C is incorrect. Since they act on different objects, they cannot cancel each other, and D is incorrect, leaving A as the correct choice.

31. B: Stretching the spring gives it some elastic potential energy. The work done is equal to the total change in energy, so this (non-zero) potential energy must be taken into account to calculate the (non-zero) work, and D is incorrect. Knowing the mass of the weight and the displacement from equilibrium is enough to find the spring constant and therefore this energy, but that information is not given! What is given is the mass of the weight, and the displacement from the equilibrium position of the hanging mass; no information is given about how much the spring stretches when the mass is first hung. The information in choice A compounds the problem; it does not provide information about the "weighted" equilibrium position, and the time provided by choice C is irrelevant. Without knowing the additional potential energy in the stretched spring (or without knowing the spring constant, from which we could calculate the potential energy), it cannot be determined how much work was done on the spring. B is therefore correct.

32. C: While the cylinder made from alloy 1 has the lowest resistance, the cylinders have different dimensions. Since conductivity is the reciprocal of resistivity, to determine which material is the best conductor, the resistivity ρ of each material can be calculated. Resistance is given by $= \frac{\rho l}{A}$, where R is the resistance of each cylinder, l is its length, and A is its cross − sectional area (equal to $\pi r2.$) Solving for $\rho = \frac{RA}{l}$ and performing this calculation for each cylinder, we find that the resistivities for alloys 1, 2, 3, and 4 are, respectively, 2.65×10^{-8} Ω·m, 5.05×10^{-8} Ω·m, 1.98×10^{-8} Ω·m, and 6.23×10^{-8} Ω·m. Of these, alloy 3 has the lowest resistivity (and therefore highest conductivity), and is therefore the best conductor.

33. C: An image in a flat mirror is upright, not inverted (upside-down), although left-to-right orientation is reversed. The image is virtual because the light rays do not actually converge at the point where the image appears and only seem to emanate from that point. One way to see this is by drawing a ray-tracing diagram like this one.

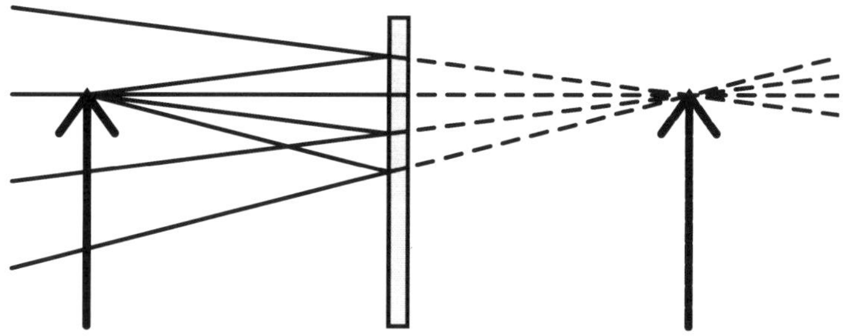

34. D: The temperature of a gas is directly proportional to the average kinetic energy of its molecules. If the temperature is increased, the molecules have a higher kinetic energy, which means they are moving at a greater speed and have more momentum. If they hit and bounce off a surface, the change in their momentum is therefore greater, and the impulse they impart to the surface is greater. Since the elapsed time of each collision with the surface does not change, the force exerted by each collision is therefore greater, and since pressure is equal to force per unit area, increasing the force applied over the same area increases the pressure of the gas. D is therefore correct.

35. 0.056 m/s: Average velocity can be calculated by dividing the displacement by the time elapsed. The dog's initial position is 40 m, and its final position is 10 m, so the displacement is 10 m – 40 m = -30 m. The total time elapsed is 9 minutes, or 540 seconds. The dog's average velocity is -30 m / 540 s = -0.056 m/s, where the negative sign indicates the overall velocity was in the direction of decreasing position. Since the question asks for average speed, the answer is 0.056 m/s.

36. B: While all the listed facts are true, only choice B is direct evidence for the dual nature of light. The other facts are readily explicable in other ways, and could be true even if light were only a wave. The fact that no electrons are emitted when the light is below a certain frequency, however, is hard to explain unless light occurs in discrete "packets". If light is strictly a continuous wave, then it should be possible to increase the intensity to compensate for the decrease in energy due to a lower frequency. That this is not the case suggests that light occurs in discrete quanta, called photons, which have energy proportional to the frequency of the light, and that each photon must have some minimum energy in order to dislodge an electron from a given material.

37. A: The formula for the gravitational force between two objects is $= \frac{Gm_1m_2}{r^2}$. Halving either m_1 or m_2 would halve the force. Halving both m_1 and m_2, however, would multiply the force by one fourth. Doubling the separation distance *r* would also multiply the force by one fourth, since that quantity is squared in the formula. For the same reason, multiplying *r* by four would multiply the force by one sixteenth! A is correct.

38. C: Conduction would require the object to be in contact with something else. (Since space isn't a *perfect* vacuum, there may actually be *some* heat lost by conduction, but the amount would not be significant.) Convection occurs within a fluid; again, it would not apply to an object floating in space. The predominant process by which such an object would lose heat is radiation; the object would radiate heat (in the form of electromagnetic radiation) into the surrounding space. All objects with a temperate greater than absolute zero emit some thermal radiation. C is the correct choice.

39. A: If there are no other acting forces, weight, like any net force, is given by mass times acceleration, in this case the acceleration due to gravity, *W=mg.* The ratio of an objects weight under Earth's gravitational acceleration to its weight under the moon's is

$$\frac{W_{Earth}}{W_{moon}} = \frac{mg_{Earth}}{mg_{moon}} = \frac{9.8\ m/s^2}{1.62\ m/s^2} = 6.05.$$

Therefore, a man with a weight of 800 N on the Earth will weigh $W_{moon} = \frac{W_{Earth}}{6.05} = \frac{800\ N}{6.05} = 132\ N$ on the moon, choice A.

40. A: When monochromatic light is diffracted through a vertical slit, it forms a horizontal (one-dimensional) pattern of light and dark bands of constructive and destructive interference between the waves of light that propagate radially from each side of the slit. Where the difference between the lengths of the paths the light waves travel from each point is an integer multiple of the wavelength of the light, the two sources interfere constructively and a bright band forms. Halfway between these points, where the difference in the path lengths is a half-integer multiple of the wavelength, the light from each point interferes destructively, leading to a dark band. The brightest band is in the center; the waves propagating from each side of the slit travel the same distance in this case, leading to strong constructive interference. The brightness of the bright bands decreases as horizontal distance increases along the screen from the point of the slit. This is depicted in choice A.

41. D: All four of these scientists contributed to the study of electromagnetism, and both Ampère and Faraday made some progress toward unifying electricity and magnetism. However, it was Maxwell who set forth the full set of equations that describe the interaction between the two aspects of the electromagnetic force, the propagation of magnetic waves, and the proof that visible light is an electromagnetic wave. These equations are therefore now generally known as Maxwell's equations.

42. C: The situation described in this problem is an example of two-dimensional projectile motion, and can be separated into its vertical and horizontal components. The symmetry of the problem can be exploited as well: half the time of the arrow's flight is spent reaching its maximum altitude, and since there is no horizontal acceleration, the arrow takes twice that time to travel the overall horizontal distance. Let's call the arrow's initial angle above the horizontal θ. The arrow's initial vertical velocity is then (80 m/s) sin θ; the arrow's vertical velocity at the top of its arc is zero. Therefore, the equation $v = v_0 + at$ yields $t_{top} = \frac{v-v_0}{a} = \frac{0\frac{m}{s}-\left(80\frac{m}{s}\right)\sin\theta}{9.8\frac{m}{s^2}} = \left(\frac{80}{9.8}\ s\right)\sin\theta$. Since t_{top} is half the total time of the flight, the total flight time $t = \left(\frac{80}{4.9}\ s\right)\sin\theta$. Let's now consider the horizontal component of the motion; the initial horizontal velocity is (80 m/s) cos θ. Since there is no horizontal acceleration, $x - x_0 = v_0t + \frac{1}{2}at^2 = v_0t$, and substituting the expression just obtained for t, $500\ m = \left(80\frac{m}{s}\right)\cos\theta\left(\frac{80}{4.9}\ s\right)\sin\theta$. A common trigonometric identity states that $2(\sin\theta)(\cos\theta) = \sin 2\theta$, which yields $500\ m = \left(\frac{80^2}{2(4.9)}\ m\right)\sin 2\theta$. Solving for θ, we get $\theta = \frac{1}{2}\sin^{-1}\left(\frac{(500)(9.8)}{80^2}\right) = 25°$.

43. D: The circumference of the rocket cars' circular path is equal to $2\pi r = 2\pi(6\ m) = 37.7$ m. Since it takes each car three seconds to travel this distance, the speed of each rocket is equal to (37.7 m)/(3 s) = 12.6 m/s. The kinetic energy of each car is therefore equal to $\frac{1}{2}mv^2 = \frac{1}{2}(500\ kg)(12.6\ m/s)^2 = 39690$ J. Since there are twelve cars, their total kinetic energy is $12(39690\ J) = 4.8\times10^5$ J.

44. B: Ultrasound is sound with a frequency above the range of human hearing. Because it has a high frequency, ultrasound actually has a low wavelength. Its velocity, though, like that of other sound waves, depends on the medium through which it travels. The ultrasound used in medical imaging typically has a frequency between 2 and 18 MHz, and is not of any particularly high amplitude. (The upper range of human hearing is about 20 kHz.) B is correct.

45. 60.0 Ω: Resistors in series sum resistances. The combined effective resistance of the two resistors on the upper wire is therefore 120 Ω + 120 Ω = 240 Ω. The same is true of the two resistors on the lower wire. The whole arrangement is therefore equivalent to three resistors in parallel, two with a resistance of 240 Ω and one (the one on the middle wire) with a resistance of 120 Ω. For resistors in parallel, the effective resistance is the reciprocal of the sum of the reciprocals of the individual resistances. Therefore, $1/R_{eff} = 1/240\ \Omega + 1/120\ \Omega + 1/240\ \Omega = 4/240\ \Omega = 1/60\ \Omega$, so the effective resistance is 60.0 Ω.

46. D: If the ship is accelerating at a constant, positive rate, then its velocity is continually increasing. The instantaneous velocity should be greatest when the most time has elapsed, in this case at t = 30 s. As for the average velocity, it can be found by taking the average of the instantaneous velocity at t = 0 s and that at t = 30 s. But since the instantaneous velocity at t = 0 s is less than that at t = 30 s, the average velocity, too, will be less than the instantaneous velocity at t = 30 s, and choice D is correct.

47. A: This problem can be solved using conservation of energy. At the top of the swing, just before he steps off the platform, the boy's kinetic energy is zero. His potential energy is equal to $mgh = m$ (9.8 m/s^2)(2.0 m) = (19.6 m^2/s^2) m. (The answer must be expressed this way, since the boy's mass is not given.) At the bottom of the swing, his potential energy is equal to $mgh = m$ (9.8 m/s^2)(0.5 m) = (4.9 m^2/s^2)m. Since the total energy is conserved, the kinetic energy he gains must be equal to the potential energy he loses, and the kinetic energy at the bottom of his swing must then be (19.6 m^2/s^2)m – (4.9 m^2/s^2)m = (14.7 m^2/s^2)m. The formula for kinetic energy is $KE = ½\ mv^2$, so $½\ mv^2$ = (14.7 m^2/s^2)m. The undetermined mass cancels, and we can solve for v to get $v = \sqrt{2(14.7\text{ m}^2/\text{s}^2)}$ = 5.4 m/s.

48. B: The amplitude is equal to the difference between the maximum displacement (for example, the height of the peak of the graph) and equilibrium. Here, equilibrium is at 0 cm, and the peak reaches 4 cm, so the amplitude is equal to (4 cm – 0 cm) = 4 cm. The x-axis (time) is irrelevant for finding the amplitude, and B is correct.

49. D: The strong nuclear force acts between quarks, and holds pairs or trios of quarks together into protons and neutrons and other particles. There is also some "left over" effect from the binding of the quarks that acts to hold together the larger particles themselves, although not as strongly as the constituent quarks are bound. It is this "residual strong force" that holds protons and neutrons together into atomic nuclei, choice D.

50. A: The easiest way to solve this problem is with the equation $v^2 = v_o^2 + 2ax$. Solving for a, this becomes $a = (v^2 - v_o^2)/2x$. In this case, v = 0 m/s (the car comes to a stop, so its final velocity is zero), v_0 = 20 m/s, and x = 40 m. So a = ((0 m/s)^2 – (20 m/s)^2)/(2(40 m)) = (-400 m^2/s^2)/(80 m) = -5 m/s^2. Only the magnitude of the acceleration is asked for, simply 5 m/s^2.

How to Overcome Test Anxiety

Just the thought of taking a test is enough to make most people a little nervous. A test is an important event that can have a long-term impact on your future, so it's important to take it seriously and it's natural to feel anxious about performing well. But just because anxiety is normal, that doesn't mean that it's helpful in test taking, or that you should simply accept it as part of your life. Anxiety can have a variety of effects. These effects can be mild, like making you feel slightly nervous, or severe, like blocking your ability to focus or remember even a simple detail.

If you experience test anxiety—whether severe or mild—it's important to know how to beat it. To discover this, first you need to understand what causes test anxiety.

Causes of Test Anxiety

While we often think of anxiety as an uncontrollable emotional state, it can actually be caused by simple, practical things. One of the most common causes of test anxiety is that a person does not feel adequately prepared for their test. This feeling can be the result of many different issues such as poor study habits or lack of organization, but the most common culprit is time management. Starting to study too late, failing to organize your study time to cover all of the material, or being distracted while you study will mean that you're not well prepared for the test. This may lead to cramming the night before, which will cause you to be physically and mentally exhausted for the test. Poor time management also contributes to feelings of stress, fear, and hopelessness as you realize you are not well prepared but don't know what to do about it.

Other times, test anxiety is not related to your preparation for the test but comes from unresolved fear. This may be a past failure on a test, or poor performance on tests in general. It may come from comparing yourself to others who seem to be performing better or from the stress of living up to expectations. Anxiety may be driven by fears of the future—how failure on this test would affect your educational and career goals. These fears are often completely irrational, but they can still negatively impact your test performance.

Elements of Test Anxiety

As mentioned earlier, test anxiety is considered to be an emotional state, but it has physical and mental components as well. Sometimes you may not even realize that you are suffering from test anxiety until you notice the physical symptoms. These can include trembling hands, rapid heartbeat, sweating, nausea, and tense muscles. Extreme anxiety may lead to fainting or vomiting. Obviously, any of these symptoms can have a negative impact on testing. It is important to recognize them as soon as they begin to occur so that you can address the problem before it damages your performance.

The mental components of test anxiety include trouble focusing and inability to remember learned information. During a test, your mind is on high alert, which can help you recall information and stay focused for an extended period of time. However, anxiety interferes with your mind's natural processes, causing you to blank out, even on the questions you know well. The strain of testing during anxiety makes it difficult to stay focused, especially on a test that may take several hours. Extreme anxiety can take a huge mental toll, making it difficult not only to recall test information but even to understand the test questions or pull your thoughts together.

Effects of Test Anxiety

Test anxiety is like a disease—if left untreated, it will get progressively worse. Anxiety leads to poor performance, and this reinforces the feelings of fear and failure, which in turn lead to poor performances on subsequent tests. It can grow from a mild nervousness to a crippling condition. If allowed to progress, test anxiety can have a big impact on your schooling, and consequently on your future.

Test anxiety can spread to other parts of your life. Anxiety on tests can become anxiety in any stressful situation, and blanking on a test can turn into panicking in a job situation. But fortunately, you don't have to let anxiety rule your testing and determine your grades. There are a number of relatively simple steps you can take to move past anxiety and function normally on a test and in the rest of life.

Physical Steps for Beating Test Anxiety

While test anxiety is a serious problem, the good news is that it can be overcome. It doesn't have to control your ability to think and remember information. While it may take time, you can begin taking steps today to beat anxiety.

Just as your first hint that you may be struggling with anxiety comes from the physical symptoms, the first step to treating it is also physical. Rest is crucial for having a clear, strong mind. If you are tired, it is much easier to give in to anxiety. But if you establish good sleep habits, your body and mind will be ready to perform optimally, without the strain of exhaustion. Additionally, sleeping well helps you to retain information better, so you're more likely to recall the answers when you see the test questions.

Getting good sleep means more than going to bed on time. It's important to allow your brain time to relax. Take study breaks from time to time so it doesn't get overworked, and don't study right before bed. Take time to rest your mind before trying to rest your body, or you may find it difficult to fall asleep.

Along with sleep, other aspects of physical health are important in preparing for a test. Good nutrition is vital for good brain function. Sugary foods and drinks may give a burst of energy but this burst is followed by a crash, both physically and emotionally. Instead, fuel your body with protein and vitamin-rich foods.

Also, drink plenty of water. Dehydration can lead to headaches and exhaustion, especially if your brain is already under stress from the rigors of the test. Particularly if your test is a long one, drink water during the breaks. And if possible, take an energy-boosting snack to eat between sections.

Along with sleep and diet, a third important part of physical health is exercise. Maintaining a steady workout schedule is helpful, but even taking 5-minute study breaks to walk can help get your blood pumping faster and clear your head. Exercise also releases endorphins, which contribute to a positive feeling and can help combat test anxiety.

When you nurture your physical health, you are also contributing to your mental health. If your body is healthy, your mind is much more likely to be healthy as well. So take time to rest, nourish your body with healthy food and water, and get moving as much as possible. Taking these physical steps will make you stronger and more able to take the mental steps necessary to overcome test anxiety.

Mental Steps for Beating Test Anxiety

Working on the mental side of test anxiety can be more challenging, but as with the physical side, there are clear steps you can take to overcome it. As mentioned earlier, test anxiety often stems from lack of preparation, so the obvious solution is to prepare for the test. Effective studying may be the most important weapon you have for beating test anxiety, but you can and should employ several other mental tools to combat fear.

First, boost your confidence by reminding yourself of past success—tests or projects that you aced. If you're putting as much effort into preparing for this test as you did for those, there's no reason you should expect to fail here. Work hard to prepare; then trust your preparation.

Second, surround yourself with encouraging people. It can be helpful to find a study group, but be sure that the people you're around will encourage a positive attitude. If you spend time with others who are anxious or cynical, this will only contribute to your own anxiety. Look for others who are motivated to study hard from a desire to succeed, not from a fear of failure.

Third, reward yourself. A test is physically and mentally tiring, even without anxiety, and it can be helpful to have something to look forward to. Plan an activity following the test, regardless of the outcome, such as going to a movie or getting ice cream.

When you are taking the test, if you find yourself beginning to feel anxious, remind yourself that you know the material. Visualize successfully completing the test. Then take a few deep, relaxing breaths and return to it. Work through the questions carefully but with confidence, knowing that you are capable of succeeding.

Developing a healthy mental approach to test taking will also aid in other areas of life. Test anxiety affects more than just the actual test—it can be damaging to your mental health and even contribute to depression. It's important to beat test anxiety before it becomes a problem for more than testing.

Study Strategy

Being prepared for the test is necessary to combat anxiety, but what does being prepared look like? You may study for hours on end and still not feel prepared. What you need is a strategy for test prep. The next few pages outline our recommended steps to help you plan out and conquer the challenge of preparation.

Step 1: Scope Out the Test

Learn everything you can about the format (multiple choice, essay, etc.) and what will be on the test. Gather any study materials, course outlines, or sample exams that may be available. Not only will this help you to prepare, but knowing what to expect can help to alleviate test anxiety.

Step 2: Map Out the Material

Look through the textbook or study guide and make note of how many chapters or sections it has. Then divide these over the time you have. For example, if a book has 15 chapters and you have five days to study, you need to cover three chapters each day. Even better, if you have the time, leave an extra day at the end for overall review after you have gone through the material in depth.

If time is limited, you may need to prioritize the material. Look through it and make note of which sections you think you already have a good grasp on, and which need review. While you are studying, skim quickly through the familiar sections and take more time on the challenging parts.

Write out your plan so you don't get lost as you go. Having a written plan also helps you feel more in control of the study, so anxiety is less likely to arise from feeling overwhelmed at the amount to cover.

Step 3: Gather Your Tools

Decide what study method works best for you. Do you prefer to highlight in the book as you study and then go back over the highlighted portions? Or do you type out notes of the important information? Or is it helpful to make flashcards that you can carry with you? Assemble the pens, index cards, highlighters, post-it notes, and any other materials you may need so you won't be distracted by getting up to find things while you study.

If you're having a hard time retaining the information or organizing your notes, experiment with different methods. For example, try color-coding by subject with colored pens, highlighters, or post-it notes. If you learn better by hearing, try recording yourself reading your notes so you can listen while in the car, working out, or simply sitting at your desk. Ask a friend to quiz you from your flashcards, or try teaching someone the material to solidify it in your mind.

Step 4: Create Your Environment

It's important to avoid distractions while you study. This includes both the obvious distractions like visitors and the subtle distractions like an uncomfortable chair (or a too-comfortable couch that makes you want to fall asleep). Set up the best study environment possible: good lighting and a comfortable work area. If background music helps you focus, you may want to turn it on, but otherwise keep the room quiet. If you are using a computer to take notes, be sure you don't have any other windows open, especially applications like social media, games, or anything else that could distract you. Silence your phone and turn off notifications. Be sure to keep water close by so you stay hydrated while you study (but avoid unhealthy drinks and snacks).

Also, take into account the best time of day to study. Are you freshest first thing in the morning? Try to set aside some time then to work through the material. Is your mind clearer in the afternoon or evening? Schedule your study session then. Another method is to study at the same time of day that you will take the test, so that your brain gets used to working on the material at that time and will be ready to focus at test time.

Step 5: Study!

Once you have done all the study preparation, it's time to settle into the actual studying. Sit down, take a few moments to settle your mind so you can focus, and begin to follow your study plan. Don't give in to distractions or let yourself procrastinate. This is your time to prepare so you'll be ready to fearlessly approach the test. Make the most of the time and stay focused.

Of course, you don't want to burn out. If you study too long you may find that you're not retaining the information very well. Take regular study breaks. For example, taking five minutes out of every hour to walk briskly, breathing deeply and swinging your arms, can help your mind stay fresh.

As you get to the end of each chapter or section, it's a good idea to do a quick review. Remind yourself of what you learned and work on any difficult parts. When you feel that you've mastered the material, move on to the next part. At the end of your study session, briefly skim through your notes again.

But while review is helpful, cramming last minute is NOT. If at all possible, work ahead so that you won't need to fit all your study into the last day. Cramming overloads your brain with more information than it can process and retain, and your tired mind may struggle to recall even previously learned information when it is overwhelmed with last-minute study. Also, the urgent nature of cramming and the stress placed on your brain contribute to anxiety. You'll be more likely to go to the test feeling unprepared and having trouble thinking clearly.

So don't cram, and don't stay up late before the test, even just to review your notes at a leisurely pace. Your brain needs rest more than it needs to go over the information again. In fact, plan to finish your studies by noon or early afternoon the day before the test. Give your brain the rest of the day to relax or focus on other things, and get a good night's sleep. Then you will be fresh for the test and better able to recall what you've studied.

Step 6: Take a Practice Test

Many courses offer sample tests, either online or in the study materials. This is an excellent resource to check whether you have mastered the material, as well as to prepare for the test format and environment.

Check the test format ahead of time: the number of questions, the type (multiple choice, free response, etc.), and the time limit. Then create a plan for working through them. For example, if you have 30 minutes to take a 60-question test, your limit is 30 seconds per question. Spend less time on the questions you know well so that you can take more time on the difficult ones.

If you have time to take several practice tests, take the first one open book, with no time limit. Work through the questions at your own pace and make sure you fully understand them. Gradually work up to taking a test under test conditions: sit at a desk with all study materials put away and set a timer. Pace yourself to make sure you finish the test with time to spare and go back to check your answers if you have time.

After each test, check your answers. On the questions you missed, be sure you understand why you missed them. Did you misread the question (tests can use tricky wording)? Did you forget the information? Or was it something you hadn't learned? Go back and study any shaky areas that the practice tests reveal.

Taking these tests not only helps with your grade, but also aids in combating test anxiety. If you're already used to the test conditions, you're less likely to worry about it, and working through tests until you're scoring well gives you a confidence boost. Go through the practice tests until you feel comfortable, and then you can go into the test knowing that you're ready for it.

Test Tips

On test day, you should be confident, knowing that you've prepared well and are ready to answer the questions. But aside from preparation, there are several test day strategies you can employ to maximize your performance.

First, as stated before, get a good night's sleep the night before the test (and for several nights before that, if possible). Go into the test with a fresh, alert mind rather than staying up late to study.

Try not to change too much about your normal routine on the day of the test. It's important to eat a nutritious breakfast, but if you normally don't eat breakfast at all, consider eating just a protein bar. If you're a coffee drinker, go ahead and have your normal coffee. Just make sure you time it so that the caffeine doesn't wear off right in the middle of your test. Avoid sugary beverages, and drink enough water to stay hydrated but not so much that you need a restroom break 10 minutes into the test. If your test isn't first thing in the morning, consider going for a walk or doing a light workout before the test to get your blood flowing.

Allow yourself enough time to get ready, and leave for the test with plenty of time to spare so you won't have the anxiety of scrambling to arrive in time. Another reason to be early is to select a good seat. It's helpful to sit away from doors and windows, which can be distracting. Find a good seat, get out your supplies, and settle your mind before the test begins.

When the test begins, start by going over the instructions carefully, even if you already know what to expect. Make sure you avoid any careless mistakes by following the directions.

Then begin working through the questions, pacing yourself as you've practiced. If you're not sure on an answer, don't spend too much time on it, and don't let it shake your confidence. Either skip it and come back later, or eliminate as many wrong answers as possible and guess among the remaining ones. Don't dwell on these questions as you continue—put them out of your mind and focus on what lies ahead.

Be sure to read all of the answer choices, even if you're sure the first one is the right answer. Sometimes you'll find a better one if you keep reading. But don't second-guess yourself if you do immediately know the answer. Your gut instinct is usually right. Don't let test anxiety rob you of the information you know.

If you have time at the end of the test (and if the test format allows), go back and review your answers. Be cautious about changing any, since your first instinct tends to be correct, but make sure you didn't misread any of the questions or accidentally mark the wrong answer choice. Look over any you skipped and make an educated guess.

At the end, leave the test feeling confident. You've done your best, so don't waste time worrying about your performance or wishing you could change anything. Instead, celebrate the successful completion of this test. And finally, use this test to learn how to deal with anxiety even better next time.

Review Video: Test Anxiety
Visit mometrix.com/academy and enter code: 100340

Important Qualification

Not all anxiety is created equal. If your test anxiety is causing major issues in your life beyond the classroom or testing center, or if you are experiencing troubling physical symptoms related to your anxiety, it may be a sign of a serious physiological or psychological condition. If this sounds like your situation, we strongly encourage you to seek professional help.

Online Resources

Due to our efforts to try to keep this book to a manageable length, we've created a link that will give you access to all of your online resources:

mometrix.com/resources719/ssregphysics

It's Your Moment, Let's Celebrate It!

Share your story @mometrixtestpreparation